All His Fingers and Toes

A story of
what a mother's love can do

Rose Weiss

Writers Club Press
San Jose New York Lincoln Shanghai

All His Fingers and Toes
A story of what a mother's love can do

Writers Club Press
an imprint of iUniverse.com, Inc.

For information address:
iUniverse.com, Inc.
620 North 48th Street
Suite 201
Lincoln, NE 68504-3467
www.iuniverse.com

ISBN: 0-595-00589-6

Printed in the United States of America

I would like to thank Leonard Nash, my literary consultant, whose creative combination of editing, proofreading, and computer talents were crucial to me as I completed the manuscript for this important book.

Chapter 1

I remember how crisp and clean the air was that Thursday morning. Summer had given way to fall, bringing brisk temperatures and a riot of glorious colors. Reds, yellows, and browns were everywhere, dressing Charleston, West Virginia in festive clothing. Maybe I was seeing the world through rose-colored glasses that day, but the city was decked out in the brightest array of autumn hues that I had ever known. It seemed as though the world had put on its best face just for me and my new husband.

I don't know if it was the beautiful autumn season that was making me giddy, or if it was simply the excitement of that special day in October 1937, but there was magic in the air and I felt alive with anticipation. Eddie and I were getting married. Married! I could hardly believe it. Eddie had just driven in from Pennsylvania for the event that would mark the beginning of the rest of our lives. No, it was going to be the beginning of the *best* of our lives. Or so we hoped.

I carefully selected my outfit carefully for that special day. I was wearing a royal blue knit dress with a matching coat and hat, and a new pair of beautiful black kid leather shoes. I felt wonderful. Buying the clothes had not been easy. After all, at the time I was earning only $12 a week working at a credit bureau. I suppose my salary amounted to a lot of money in those days, but I was helping to support my family. I learned early on that life wouldn't always be easy.

So Eddie and I were married in the Rabbi's study at Temple Israel in the late afternoon. It was a small wedding with just the immediate family in attendance. I was told that our wedding dinner at the Daniel Boone Hotel was delicious, but I'll never know. The new Mrs. Eddie Weiss was too excited to sit down and eat.

But as we laughed and danced in celebration of this miraculous event, night crept upon us, bringing with it a tempestuous storm of huge proportions. The unexpected wind roared and the rain raged outside, flooding Charleston. Drivers were told to stay off the streets. The deluge had made it impossible to navigate the roadways safely. We were at the mercy of Mother Nature, stranded and unable to make our way out into the world. But we were young and in love and so it didn't matterCnot on that night. We spent our honeymoon at the Daniel Boone Hotel, wrapped in the security of each other's arms as the storm spent itself outside.

Then Friday morning arrived bright and clear. Our families continued the celebration of our marriage with gatherings for lunch and dinner. Then, on Saturday, we waved goodbye to everyone and drove off in a shower of rice and a hail of tin cans trailing our car. I was leaving West Virginia behind to start my married life in a new home in California, Pennsylvania, a small town about 30 miles southwest of Pittsburgh, where Eddie had opened a small drugstore.

We began our marriage with enthusiasm. Eddie was a pharmacist and we owned one of the two drugstores in town. I eagerly assisted my new husband in our cheerful, small-town emporium with its curious mix of bottles and jars, candy displays full with barrels of jelly beans and lollipops, aisles filled with office stationary, toiletries, and so forth. We even had an ice cream fountain which attracted the neighborhood children on their way home from school. I loved being at the store, and found myself wanting to spend as much time there as possible.

For the 1930's, California, PA was a typical small college town with a population of about 15,000. The beginning days of our marriage were grand as we put things together for our new home, an upstairs apartment about half a mile from the drugstore. We walked to and from work, arm in arm, chatting and dreaming, proudly greeting our friends and neighbors. The distance never seemed more than an easy trek in a town where nearly everyone did a lot of walking.

And so we spent our days loving each other and thinking of the future. Of course the future included furnishings, so our first project of married life became the outfitting of our apartment. Driving into Pittsburgh was an adventure for us. We shopped, chose, and arranged for the delivery of creature comforts into our home. Our bedroom furnishings had been provided as part of the rental, but we added living room and kitchen furniture. Once the apartment had taken shape, we marveled at what we had accomplished. Together, out of bare walls and rooms, we had created a home.

Even Eddie, who as the years passed often failed to "stop and smell the roses" as they say, would later look back and confess that our small town never looked lovelier than it did during those early fall days of 1938. The great oak trees spread their spacious, leafy arms and shaded us against the sun as we walked along the beautiful broad avenues. Never did I enjoy blue skies, birds chirping, and children playing in the streets and yards more than during those warm days.

Just a few months after we were married, we experienced the joy of learning that I was "expecting," as we called it in those days. Immediately, Eddie and I began to plan for the arrival of what we hoped would be many children. We decorated the small room just off our bedroom with a new white crib and a shining little chest of drawers and we hung cheerful animal curtains in the window.

Eddie was the youngest of a large Hungarian family and I was one five children, so parenthood was something we looked forward to without any hesitation. Children were considered a blessing and ours would be no exception.

Eddie and I couldn't wait to become parents. Sometimes we would stay up late, holding each other, talking about our dreams for this and our other children yet to be. We were sure this first baby would have

blonde, curly hair like Eddie had as a baby. Eddie daydreamed of toss-
ing baseballs to his son in the spring and lobbing a football to him in
the fall. I envisioned my daughter at her first piano recital, dressed in
lace and ribbon. Of course we really didn't care if our baby was a boy or
a girl. All we knew was that having a baby would be wonderful. In less
than a year, our marriage had taken on a purpose beyond anything we
had ever imagined. We were going to become a family.

We had so much fun picking names for the baby. Because Eddie was
so convinced that the baby was going to be a boy, male names were the
only names he would consider. After many weeks of discussion, we
finally agreed on Elliott for a boy. And if it were a girl, we decided that
we would name her Marlene.

Eddie stood on the stool in the small room just off our bedroom,
twisting his jaw with grim determination as he gave the screwdriver a
last half-turn to secure the drapery rod. I sat on the chair next to the
glistening white crib, admiring him while he worked.

Eddie didn't look his age, but he was thirty, six years older than me,
and at five foot five, he was almost six inches taller. Eyeglasses and a
thick mustache helped him look a little older, but his slight frame, boyish complexion, and jet black wavy hair worked against him. He looked
like a teenager working to wind up an overdue shop project and I was
the cheerleader he had gotten in trouble. Our next door neighbor said
we looked as though we were playing house. I liked playing house with
Eddie. As this story will describe, we would later find ourselves endur-
ing many difficult years, and so I am glad that I've been able to hold
those idyllic moments in my memory all these many years later.

Eddie came down off the stool to admire his handiwork and cast a
skeptical eye at the animal pattern on the curtains that were going up
on the rod. I knew he wasn't very happy with them, but they were the
curtains I had chosen. With a laugh, Eddie said they were going to come
down the very day our son was ready for football practice. I responded

with the fact that the baby could be a girl who would someday be ready for her first piano recital! Either way, it didn't matter whether it was a boy or a girl. The baby was welcome and it would be loved.

Eddie started to pick up the curtains but stopped and picked me up from my chair, giving me a bear hug. I squeezed him back, enjoying the strength of his arms around me. My stomach got in the way, but it didn't matter. Eddie never said much during our intimate moments. Looking back, I suppose he never said much at all. He was the youngest of thirteen children and I was the youngest of five. Children from such large families don't have many opportunities for long speeches. I liked actions better than words anyway.

Then Eddie went back to the curtains and I went back to the crib, inspecting it for the hundredth time that day. It was almost time. There were crisp sheets on the mattress and soft little clothes in the white dresser. The cot was set up in the corner for a nurse, and the bathinette was firmly in place by the kitchen sink. I couldn't think of anything else we needed.

Impulsively, I picked up one of the white cotton nightgowns from the dresser drawer and ran it across my cheek. I could almost feel the silky sheen of my baby and smell the fresh essence of a newborn child. It put an eager knot of anticipation in my stomach and the baby responded with a kick.

"She's kicking, Eddie," I announced, feeling the place with my hand.

"He's kicking, Rose," Eddie said. And he came down off the stool to kiss me again.

The next morning, bright and early as usual, Eddie left for the pharmacy, hurrying lightly down the outside steps from our apartment to the tree-lined street. And once I finished the breakfast dishes, I also left for the store. It was fall and the leaves of the enormous oak trees that lined the streets of our town were once again turning the colors of fall. I took my time taking my regular route along the sidewalk to the store, watching the geese wing noisily southward over the treetops, admiring the foliage, and, most of all, watching the children.

The town of California, PA had lots of children. The older ones were already in school, but the toddlers were out in force on their lawns. They were vigorously propelling tricycles at breakneck speeds down sloping front walkways and careening dangerously onto the sidewalk at the last instant before hurtling into the streets. A two-year-old whizzed past my legs, oblivious, making a siren sound as he sped away on an imaginary errand. I turned and watched him disappear around the corner of the block, his short, strong legs expertly powering him forward.

The door chime jangled as I entered the store. Eddie was in the back, at the pharmacy counter, talking with Dr. Wilson, who maintained a practice upstairs. They came to the front together and greeted me.

"How's the mother doing?" Dr. Wilson asked. He had white hair and ruddy cheeks that were laced with thin red lines from ruptured vessels. He wore a dark suit and had his stethoscope dangling from his neck.

"I'm doing just fine, Doctor," I told him. "We've got everything ready for you at home."

"Good. Good. Shouldn't be long now. Are you getting the Braxton-Hicks contractions? False labor?"

"Nothing regular, not yet."

"Well, just call me when you start getting the pains 10 to 15 minutes apart or if your water breaks. Doesn't matter what time of day it is, I'll be right over." He gave me a fatherly pat on the shoulder. "Got to take care of you or Eddie won't fill my prescriptions."

"We've got faith in you," Eddie told him.

"Good. Good. Then I'll see you on Thursday for your check-up Rose, if not before."

He laughed good-naturedly, perhaps at a joke only he could hear, and started for the door.

"It *will* be all right, having the baby at home, won't it, doctor?" He stopped halfway through the doorway and looked back at me, laughing again. "Don't you worry, Rose. I've delivered at least a thousand babies by now. You won't have a thing to worry about." And then Dr. Wilson was gone.

I looked at Eddie. "I just wish it was over already," I said. "The waiting seems so long."

Eddie smiled reassuringly. "You have to be patient, Rose."

Chapter 2

"He's not breathing."

These were the first words I heard as my child made his ominously silent entrance into the world. As I looked around see what was happening, I silently prayed that I had not heard correctly. It could not be my baby! I saw the doctor move rapidly and I held my breath as he put his mouth on the infant's lips, breathing quickly in and out in attempt to infuse life into the tiny body which was so deathly still. But then, suddenly, my baby began breathing rhythmically, properly, and I also took a deep breath, trying to calm down and convince myself that everything was all right.

Dr. Wilson lifted the baby boy by his legs and spanked him lightly on the buttocks to get the customary first cry, but the baby remained silent. And then there was movement. A tiny leg jerked and extended to full length. I caught the new hope in nurse Sarah's eyes and clung to this thought. Dr. Wilson rose slightly again, and the tiny creature in his hands waved angry fists at him. But still he made no sound. No sound! Newborn babies cried. Even with my very limited experience, I knew this for a fact. Why wasn't my son crying? How could I tell my husband that our new son was not perfect?

It was early evening on September 8, 1938 and Elliott, my first born, had arrived. He was bathed, dressed, and handed to me to be admired. He looked so angelic, his face like a cherub, his eyes bright and alert. I could not detect anything about him that was not perfect in shape or form. He had all his fingers and toes. I knew for sure because I had examined each one and had counted them several times.

Eddie sat by the side of the bed and tenderly pulled back the receiving blanket to glimpse a better look at his son's face.

"Eddie, he's so quiet. You don't think he's mute?"

"Rose, he's not mute." Eddie made little cooing noises at the child cradled in my arms. "He'll cry soon enough…Just look at him, Rose. Have you ever seen a better looking baby?"

I knew that newborns take some time to get over the trauma of birth before they start to look cute, but Elliott was an exception. From the blonde fuzz on the top of his head to the tiny toes on each foot, he seemed like a normal, healthy, perfect baby. He had a round face, good color, very few wrinkles, and his eyes were wide open. And each time I saw my beautiful baby son, my heart reached out to him with love and kindness.

The first few times I tried to feed Elliott, I offered him the prepared formula Dr. Wilson had prescribed, but much to my dismay, Elliott was unable to get his lips around the nipple, and when he tried, it kept falling from his mouth. In vain, I repeatedly tried to breast feed. Tears formed in my eyes. I asked myself, "Why were my baby and I being punished?" We had done nothing wrong. I took all the vitamins regularly and ate the right foods during my pregnancy. I did not drink or smoke. So why were we being punished?

I asked Sarah, the nurse, to please bring me an eyedropper and fill it with milk. To our joy, it worked! Part of the milk dribbled onto Elliott's chin, but he did retain some, at least enough to sustain him. This would be the first of many challenges and creative solutions that we were about to encounter.

It was forty-eight hours before Elliott began to utter his first cry. Those early frantic wails filled our house like a joyous symphony. I said a deep prayer and reassured myself that now everything would be all right.

After Elliott's nap the next day, Sarah brought Elliott to me to be nursed; however, she had a concerned look on her face. Elliott had a strange, brownish-yellow cast to the whites of his eyes and his flesh was not the beautiful pink it had been at birth. Sarah said it looked like jaundice. She maintained that Elliott's liver was not mature enough yet and that he needed more sunlight.

For nine months you live with your child growing inside you, and so your entire being centers around your hopes and aspirations for this new life that you will give to the world. It is impossible for a mother to conceive anything but a perfect image, and when this image becomes reality it must conform, in every way, to the ideal you have established. Any inconsistency becomes enormous.

I should have faith in our doctor, I kept repeating in my mind. He told me the baby was fine; that he was healthy and would grow up to be happy and tall and wonderful. Despite the doctor's optimistic words, I was still afraid.

The jaundice lasted for three weeks. During that time I experienced every doubt and fear a mother could conjure up. Perhaps it would have been easier to cope if he had possessed an abnormality that I could see or an illness that I could understand. Instead, my child had a quiet discontent that was shaped by my imagination into horrible life-threatening maladies. Everyone tried to help me. Eddie would sit by my bedside, hold my hand, and tell me what a wonderful child we have, but I could always hear the doubts in his voice. Sarah was stead-fast in her determination that Elliott was normal, but I did not believe her either. A mother knows these things.

At the end of the week, Dr. Wilson returned to check on us. He exam-ined the baby carefully, shining lights in his eyes, testing his reflexes, prob-ing his skin with his fingertips. Dr. Wilson was smiling when he came to me. He promised me that everything was going to be all right. He said, "I must admit that Elliott is a little slow getting started, but I still believe that he is going to be a fine, healthy child. The respiration problem he had in the beginning is holding him back a little. But that is all."

How I wished that Dr. Wilson was right! But, Elliott wasn't just a slow baby. There was something wrong and it became increasingly clear in the frequent trips I made to the doctor's office in the weeks that followed.

So many times I have heard mothers declare that they wish their children would be more quiet or less of a bother to them, but I was praying for my child to make a fuss and to stop being such a "perfect baby." He slept constantly, and most of his waking hours were quiet ones. But he was also beautiful and I clung to my faint hopes that my worries were unfounded. Such a handsome infant could not possibly have anything seriously wrong with him.

Looking back, and even at the time, I've wondered if things might have turned out differently for Elliott if he had been born in the hospital, but that was not always an option in the late 1930's, particularly in a town as small as California, PA. Most of Eddie's pharmacy business came from Dr. Wilson, one of the busiest physicians in town, and so it wouldn't have been prudent to have another doctor deliver our child. Eddie insisted that Dr. Wilson was a qualified physician, but I kept having terrible nagging doubts, and our child's lack of progress soon backed them up.

Elliott had weighed 7 pounds, 14 ounces at birth. Because we weren't feeding him from a bottle or the breast at first, Elliott gained weight slowly. When he tried to eat, he often gagged on the formula, which caused him to retain only a small portion of his food. I suspected that this was the heart of the problem. When Elliott was about a month old, we were elated when he finally learned to swallow his food, and in a short time, he grew 2-1/2 inches and gained 3 pounds. There was hope.

When Sarah's month with us came to an end, she took a position to care for another newborn. Now Elliott was solely in my care. I tried to make him hold a rattle and play with his nursery toys, but he could not grasp them, nor did he show any interest in them. This made us more

aware of a possible muscle handicap. It was then that I began to wonder if Elliott would ever sit, walk, or talk.

During the next few months, Elliott still showed no interest in his
toys or rattles. I became more alarmed as he did not show the normal
desires of babies. At night I would lie awake and worry. "What was his
future going to be like? How could I help?"

On our long outings in the crisp air, I constantly showed Elliott the
beautiful leaves and explained the different colors to him. We had one-
way conversations, but I didn't care. He was all I had to talk to during
these walks and I believe he heard me, despite his inability to respond.
Our walks usually led us to see daddy at the drugstore where we would
say hello to the customers.

Dressed in his white bunting suit, Elliott looked like a doll. But a
closer look would reveal that he was tied into the carriage and propped
up from behind with a pillow; otherwise, his body slumped over and his
head flopped about uncontrollably. Even when carrying my baby
around the house, I supported his little head by cupping it with the
palm of my hand. Inwardly, I prayed Elliott would awaken one day soon
and be perfectly normal. Instead, the days stretched into months and
Elliott's problems became more evident.

The ritual circumcision, or bris, which is customarily performed on
Jewish boys at the age of seven days old, was delayed because of Elliott's
abnormality. But finally, at six weeks old, the doctor decided it should
take place. With all of Elliott's feeding problems, he now had to be con-
fronted with a surgical procedure. I was against doing it, but Eddie and
other men in the family insisted that the procedure was customary and
that it had to be done.

It was a very emotional day. Our small apartment overflowed with
family and friends. We selected Eddie's brother, Uncle Emil, to be the
godfather, so it was his privilege to hold Elliott during the circumcision.

Eddie's mother took care of all the arrangements. She prepared the food and brought her housemaid to serve and clean up.

Elliott let out a loud cry when the foreskin was cut; however, a few moments later, with wine spattered on his lips, he quietly went to sleep and all was calm. When he fell asleep, I was bombarded with questions about his eating and sleeping habits and about what progress he was making. With each answer I became more and more disturbed. I wanted everyone to vanish quickly. I did not want more questions for which I had no answers, only doubts.

I didn't know what month a baby is first expected to hold a rattle or kick his feet or sleep through the night. I was a new mother. I had to learn from experience. I had not read any books about babies. I thought motherhood came naturally. I thought motherhood brought daily joy.

Chapter 3

When Elliott was about eight months old, I hired a professional photographer to take some portrait-style photographs. I was busy in the kitchen when I heard a sharp rapping on the front door. I found the photographer standing on the front porch, grinning broadly while he struggled to hold up an awkward collection of reflectors, lights, and tripods.

"Mrs. Weiss? Good morning! I'm from the studio."

"Yes, we've been expecting you," I said holding open the screen door. "Please come in."

The man started through the doorway, banged his Graflex on the frame, re-angled, and entered calmly on the second try. With cords dangling and tripods rattling loudly, he struggled into the living room and gratefully surrendered his burden onto the couch. Brushing his hands together with satisfaction, he looked around the room.

"There now. Where's our subject?"

"I'll get him. Would you like some coffee?"

"When I'm finished, thanks. It'll only take a minute."

I hesitated nervously and went into the nursery, lifting Elliott from his crib. I had already dressed him in his best outfit and he looked at me with anticipation as I carried him into the living room. The photographer came over, smiling, and inspected his newest client.

"Well, aren't you a good-looking fellow? Maybe we'll send your portrait off to Gerber so they can put you on their cereal boxes." He laughed at his own joke, a joke he probably made dozens of times per month. He tweaked Elliott's cheek, and then he was all business. "OK, Mrs. Weiss, we'll sit him on a table over here by the window, and I'll place the backdrop over here."

"Fine," I said hesitantly. "I'll get the blanket."

"Oh, we won't need that, ma'am. I've got all the props."

"You don't understand," I insisted. "I'll need the blanket to support him from behind. So you won't see my hands."

He looked at me strangely. "How old is your boy?"

"Eight months."

"Then he can hold his head up just fine. It'll be all right. We know what we're doing," he said, suddenly referring to himself in the plural tense. We've photographed a million kids just his age."

I've never understood why people retreat into the editorial "we" when they're trying to explain that they know more about something than you do? It's a habit I've noticed in crooked politicians and befuddled appliance repairmen. Before I could say another word, the photographer hustled off to set up the backdrop and the lights. I followed him, still persistent.

"I'm afraid you don't understand. Elliott's a slow child. He has difficulty doing things for himself." I realized as I said it that I'd never used the term "slow" before to refer to my son.

"Sitting up comes naturally, Mrs. Weiss. He can do it fine on his own. No need to be overprotective. Just watch." The man put the backdrop in place, whisked Elliott from my arms, and carried him to the waiting table.

"All right, captain, we want you to sit right here and smile for the little birdie," he commanded. He sat Elliott on the table and immediately, Elliott doubled over. "Come on, son. Sit up for me." There was a note of exasperation in the photographer's voice. "No time to fall asleep now. Sit up for the camera."

Elliott's head rolled uncontrollably.

"Come on, boy." The man's face was beginning to wrinkle with impatience. It was apparent that Elliott wasn't going to respond for him. He looked at me. "I suppose there is something wrong with your boy, Mrs. Weiss."

There was no longer any question. Elliott had smiled at three weeks and laughed at three months. He could drink from a cup, and by all outward appearances he was normal, yet he had no control over his body. He couldn't hold up his head or sit unaided. And at times when other babies would have started crying, Elliott was still as languid as a newborn. As the pictures were being taken, I propped Elliott up, holding him in place, my hands under his blanket, just as Eddie and I had done when taking our amateur snapshots.

I wasn't lacking from advice on ways to help Elliott. Everyone had a formula.

Later that month, Eddie's mother visited from Monessen, a nearby city where one of his brothers was living. Recently widowed, she was a short, imposing woman with the authority of having raised thirteen children of her own, as well as innumerable grandchildren. She carried the conviction of her Hungarian upbringing and an intense aura of command as she entered the house and settled into a living room chair.

"Bring me my grandson," she said, and Eddie rushed to bring forth Elliott and lay him in her arms. She bounced the child lightly against her breast for a moment, looking at him skeptically. Elliott's head rolled wildly in her arms.

"His muscles are too loose," she announced, as though it were something that had escaped our attention.

"We know, Mama," Eddie told her. "He's not coming along very fast."

"He needs starch," she proclaimed.

"Starch?" I asked, thinking that she meant Hungarian pasta or potatoes.

"Starch," she repeated. "Rose, you must bathe him in starch water. Potato starch. It will make him stiff like the collar of a new shirt. Do it often and he'll be well. I know. It's what we did in the Old Country."

At least Eddie's mother could suggest a cure, no matter how misdirected or confused. Dr. Wilson was much less help. I could see that he was becoming increasingly uncomfortable with my regular visits to his office. His routine showed little variation. He would take Elliott's temperature, stretch his arms and legs, and peer into the baby's eyes. Always, at the end of the examination, he would shake his head and then tell me the same sort of nonsense: "He should start coming around now, Mrs. Weiss. He's a healthy baby. Just still a little slow."

The morning, after one of these examinations, I planned my next course of action. With breakfast on the table, I waited with anticipation while Eddie finished his shachrit, the morning prayers, in the bedroom. I formed my argument carefully while I waited, listening for the sound of his footsteps coming from the bedroom. He reached the doorway of the kitchen and stopped for a moment, suddenly clutching the door frame and shaking his head.

"Eddie, what's wrong?"

He waved me off with his hand.

"It's nothing. I got up too quick and it made me a little dizzy." Eddie didn't look all right. His color was flushed.

"You're sure? Eddie, you don't look like you feel well. All we need is for you to get sick now."

"I'm all right." He smiled reassuringly and came over to the breakfast table. I studied him carefully as he sat down and took the first sip of coffee, the color beginning to flow back into his cheeks.

"You didn't sleep well last night, either, Eddie."

"My stomach was bothering me. Probably just a touch of the flu."

"It's been happening a lot lately."

"Please, Rose. It's nothing." From the tone in his voice I could tell that he didn't want to talk about it any further, but he knew I wasn't going to let him off that easily. He added, as an insincere concession, "If it gets any worse, I'll ask Dr. Wilson about it."

"Dr. Wilson is what I want to talk to you about," I said, deciding to go ahead with my original plan. I sat down across from Eddie at the table. "I don't think he's helping Elliott."

Eddie began to spoon his cereal. He wasn't looking at me.

"He's delivered and raised a lot of healthy children, Rose."

"But he's not helping ours. I know he's a good friend, Eddie, and an important client of ours, but what if he's not good enough to help Elliott? What if he feels guilty about something that happened when the baby was born? Perhaps he gave me too much medication to induce labor, or he maybe he shouldn't have tried so hard to get Elliott to breathe at first. Couldn't he have known that there might be damage later on?"

Eddie looked at me sharply. "Rose, that's a terrible thing to say. Wilson's a good man and a very well-respected doctor."

"I know, Eddie, I know," I said. The tears I didn't want forced their way into my eyes. "I know he's a good man, Eddie, but he just hasn't been good enough. I want someone else to look at our son before it's too late."

Eddie went back to his cereal, chasing it around the bowl with his spoon, but he wasn't eating. Finally, he nodded. "Maybe a second opinion won't hurt, so long as you don't see another doctor here in town. Dr. Wilson doesn't need to know about our private business."

"Let's take him to Pittsburgh. There's good doctors there."

"Absolutely," Eddie said. "I'll make some calls and see if I can't get us the name of a good pediatrician in the city."

"Let's do it, Eddie, right away, while we can still help our son."

Eddie came up with a lot of names in the weeks that followed, but most of them were pediatricians with small office practices, and in their own way they were as knowledgeable and helpful as Dr. Wilson. We would go for an examination, then sit in an endless series of wood-paneled offices while kindly doctors reclined in their leather executive chairs or perched on the corner of immense oak desks to give us their verdicts. Each doctor had a different opinion: muscular problems, malnutrition, nervous ailments, bone diseases. None of these ideas rang true, but we tried each of their suggestions for treatment: large doses of vitamins, a sun lamp, rigid diets, and countless other remedies. They all had the same effect, or lack thereof.

"At first, Eddie was tolerant of the interminable series of tests and examinations. Although he didn't speak much, he confessed that Elliott needed more help. He would often sit by our son's crib watching him, and he would say, "I just don't understand how the Lord could do this to such a beautiful child." In this matter, we agreed wholeheartedly.

I didn't realize how much the stress of the situation was troubling Eddie until one night at supper when he confessed that he had been in to see Dr. Wilson for his own problems. He produced a small brown bottle and popped a white lozenge into his mouth as he began eating.

"What's that, Eddie?" Always the pharmacist, he explained it to me with a twenty-syllable technical name.

"No, really," I insisted. What is it?"

"A tranquilizer," he said, shuffling his food around on his plate moodily. "Wilson gave it to me for my stomach problem and the dizzy spells."

"What's wrong, Eddie?" I asked urgently.

"Nothing organic, Rose. Don't worry yourself. It's only stress."

"Is something wrong at work?"

"Oh, just the usual." He nodded toward the high chair where Elliott had been strapped into place, supported by a pillow, while we ate. "I just worry about him too much, I guess. Dr. Wilson wants me to relax a little more."

Eddie turned to his food again, making it clear that this was all that we were going to discuss about the matter. Elliott gurgled beside him, his bright eyes staring at his father.

I had not realized the reassurances I demanded from Eddie, or that I had pressured him so greatly when he put on his strong, comforting facade. In general, our home life had been good over the last year. The house was frequently filled with friends and relatives who seemed to overlook Elliott's misfortunes as they showered their affection upon him. We even took turns baby-sitting so that each of us could enjoy an occasional night out. Prior to this, Eddie never let on that our son's affliction was eating away at him. But that night, I came to realize that Elliott's problems were a constant emotional burden to him, just as they were for me.

Elliott and I visited the store every day, and it seemed to take some of the pressure off Eddie. He would lift Elliott out of the carriage and carry him down the aisles of bright packages and exotic-looking bottles. I stood by the counter, watching my son enjoy the daily inventory with his father.

"Well, what do you think of this dusty old drugstore, boy? Do you like all the pretty bottles?" Elliott cooed contentedly. "See that? Mom puts that stuff on her fingernails." Eddie grabbed for the bottle. "No, no, sorry, not for you. Look over here. See that? Jellybeans. Pretty Soon you can have one. What do you think of that? Which one would you like?"

The front door jangled as a customer wandered into the store. Eddie looked up at him, smiling, still holding Elliott.

"Good morning, sir. Can I help you?"

"Well, I'll be," the man said, only half joking. "This is a real baby."

"Yes," Eddie said quietly. "He's my son."

"I never would have known. He stays so beautiful and still. Just passing by and looking through the window, I would have thought it was a little doll you were holding." The man tickled Elliott under the chin and wandered off down an aisle. I could see the resignation wash over Eddie's face. Silently, he handed Elliott back to me and went back behind the pharmacy counter. The stress was still there, and the lack of knowing anything conclusive weighed heavily on all of us. But if none of the doctors understood, what could we do? Before long it, we knew it would be impossible to hide the fact that Elliott was handicapped.

It was a bitter word, but I was beginning to use it more and more often in my mind. There was something less than normal about our son. When a person is afflicted, one must first learn the name of the malady that possesses him in order to fight it. We felt that way with Elliott, and if we could only put a label on the problem, then maybe we could defeat it. Instead, we had a beautiful child who wasn't progressing, who remained flaccid, but usually smiled in our arms.

I strapped Elliott into the carriage and was ready to head out when a regular customer entered the store. It was a man wearing a herringbone overcoat over a three-piece suit. He pushed a teenage boy before him in a large wicker carriage. The boy's head rolled unnaturally to the side, like Elliott's, and his hands and legs were twisted at odd angles. The man smiled sheepishly at me and directed his son over to the ice cream counter. I stood rooted to the spot, watching as he ordered a dish of vanilla ice cream and then patiently spooned it into his son's mouth, wiping away the drool that inevitably spilled out. Feeling weak, I turned back to Eddie and saw he had been watching as well. My eye caught his and he turned away, retreating to the back of the store.

Our son will never be like that, or have to be fed by someone, I told myself, looking down at Elliott in the stroller. But first we had to find out what was wrong and deal with it. There just wasn't any other way.

A few weeks later I bought a new stroller with a metal plate on the bottom where a child could rest his feet, but Elliott was already a little big for it, so I removed the plate and left him sitting in the stroller in the living room. The first time I put him into it, he was still for a moment, and then he stretched his foot out tentatively to touch the floor. His tiny shoe pressed against the rug as if testing it, and then surprisingly, he shoved. The stroller moved a few inches backward. Elliott giggled and looking around. He stretched his foot out again and shoved again. The stroller rolled slowly toward the couch and bounced to a stop.

Elliott was propped up with a pillow, but he could look around. His brow wrinkled in concentration and he shoved again, this time moving the stroller at a slight angle from the couch.

The back door opened and Eddie came in, exhausted from a long day at the store. He saw me standing transfixed in the living room entrance and came over curiously to see what was going on.

"He's moving, Eddie," I told him. "Elliott's moving on his own."

Elliott grunted and shoved again, and the stroller went forward this time. He trundled over to the coffee table and began diligently exploring. Eddie and I looked at one another in amazement.

Yes. For the first time, Elliott was moving about on his own. It was a start.

Chapter 4

Elliott pushed his stroller around the corner of one of the drugstore aisles, saw what he was looking for, and homed in on it. Sticking his tongue out of the corner of his mouth with determination, he navigated between the magazine racks and shampoo bottles to the large barrel of jellybeans at the candy counter. As he reached the candy counter, he came to a bumping stop and then stretched over the top to scoop out a handful of jellybeans. Oblivious to everything happening around him, he awkwardly drew in his prize, holding it in his lap while he picked out the black beans first, chewing them with obvious delight.

"That shows he can pick out colors and demonstrate a preference," Eddie told me from our vantage point by the pharmacy counter. "And he's getting around better. Maybe he'll be normal after all."

"He still needs help, Eddie," I insisted. "Aunt Tillie and Uncle Julius want me to go see a doctor they know in Miami. He's an orthopedist. Tillie and Julius wouldn't have recommended him if they didn't think he might be able to help. They love Elliott very much."

"Florida is a long way," Eddie replied doubtfully. "I don't know if I want you going so far away."

"It's for Elliott's sake, Eddie. If there's a way to help him, we have to try it."

"Are you sure you're not just sick of the Pennsylvania winter?"

"The winters here are difficult," I conceded, "but it's Elliott that I'm concerned about, Eddie. He's so sickly...I think Miami will be good for him."

Eddie's fingertips drummed on the counter as he thought about it.

"Well, maybe. We've tried everything else. And you need a vacation. As long as you don't get in the habit."

And as we continued to struggle with Elliott's mysterious deformities, events were taking an ominous turn in the rest of the world. President Roosevelt had gone against the nationwide isolationist sentiments to ask Congress to provide a Lend-Lease program to aid the Allies, and at the same time he submitted a mammoth $17.5 billion budget to Congress that included $11 billion for defense. It seemed as though the government knew it would be drawn into war. In response, many influential senators and business leaders had joined together to establish the America First Committee in an attempt to keep us out of the war, although it meant abandoning our nation's friends overseas and, in particular, the millions of Jews we knew Hitler was persecuting in the occupied countries.

The threat of war was driving prices upward rapidly, making it doubly hard to meet our payments for Elliott's tuition. Eddie had difficulty stocking many of the items that were normally carried in the store, from chocolate to important medicines.

Despite the adversity, the country seemed bursting with hope and creativity. Production was picking up, partly due to the large defense expenditures, and the Depression was, at last, truly over. Americans were responding with fantastic works, from the stone heads of Mount Rushmore, to the great literary works that were beginning to emerge. F. Scott Fitzgerald had died the previous December, leaving behind *The Last Tycoon*, which was just being published posthumously, sharing the shelf with *What Makes Sammy Run?* and *The Keys to the Kingdom*Call reflecting new faith in the economy or the magnitude of power at the top. *Citizen Kane, The Maltese Falcon,* and *Sergeant York* were showing at the movies, and the radio was playing AChattanooga Choo-Choo," "The Boogie-Woogie Bugle Boy," and AThe Jersey Bounce." It was a bold, bright time before the gathering darkness.

It was a cold, drizzly day when we boarded the train in Pittsburgh. Soldiers and sun-bound tourists filled the passenger cars and the brilliant domed observatories. Elliott chortled with excitement as the train pulled from the station and the panorama outside the windows began to unfold. As we passed houses, farms, and small villages, I told Elliott stories about them as he watched in wide-eyed amazement.

"Do you see that farm? It's Old MacDonald's farm. See his horses? Do you know what kind of sound those cows make? Moo-oo."

Elliott laughed happily and bounced on my knee, supported from behind by my carefully placed hand. Across the aisle, fellow travelers smiled warmly at him. Despite his excitement, the gentle rocking of the train soon lulled him to sleep, and by the time the warm morning light streamed through the windows, we were in Florida. An entirely new vista of palm trees and palmetto shrub stretched around us. Cattle grazed on open plains, and the sky was clearer and brighter than it ever seemed in Pennsylvania.

As we stepped out into the warm, invigorating air at the train station in Miami, Tillie and Julius were there to meet us. They grabbed Elliott from me and squeezed him with genuine affection, and he burbled back a happy sound in response, his arms and legs flailing in a worm-like, disjointed manner.

"It's good to see you, little one," Julius told Elliott. "We've got a man here who is going to make you all better. What do you think of that?"

His eyes sparkled with confidence as he said it, and Tillie patted my hand comfortingly. I tried to share their enthusiasm, but as always the doubt and apprehension plagued me.

We unwound for a few days before making our appointment with Dr. Kaiser. He gave Elliott one of the most thorough examinations the boy had ever had, while I hung back, trying to keep out of the way. Finally, we were led into his office and offered a chair.

"Please sit down, Mrs. Weiss. I think you were wise to bring Elliott down to see us."

"Can you help him?"

"I'm afraid it's impossible to tell you anything definite. Any sort of prognosis we could make for your son would be based largely on guesswork. The boy's determination will ultimately decide how much he will be able to accomplish, particularly in the area of expressive language."

I felt my hopes sinking yet again, but at least Dr. Kaiser hadn't mentioned a physical disability. It would be all right, somehow, even if he couldn't talk, if he could only get about by himself. He was doing so well with the stroller…

"What about walking, doctor?"

"There again, it's difficult to say. Certainly physical therapy would help and it should be started as soon as possible. There's an excellent man down here I want to refer to you. His name is Dayton, O.W. Dayton, and he is extremely dedicated. If anyone can see to it that Elliott walks on his own, Dr. Dayton should be able to help."

Once Dr. Dayton had examined Elliott, I asked, ABut what's the problem, doctor? Why can't he walk? What's holding him back?"

Dr. Dayton began to study his notes with a sudden interest. "I can't really say for sure. It's a difficult case, and the cause doesn't really matter. What we have to do now is find a way to make him better."

Dayton's advice turned out to be the first positive suggestion anyone had given us, and despite the cost, we enrolled Elliott in a therapy program five days a week. He worked with Elliott slowly, placing him on the matted floor and drawing one leg forward, then an arm, then another leg, then the other arm, always offering words of encouragement.

"There you go, Elliott. You can do it. Just a little more. One leg at a time. That's better."

And Elliott did it. As I watched, he put out one hesitant arm on his own, then followed with his leg, gradually hoisting his tiny body behind him. He was crawling.

Within a month, with daily encouragement from the dedicated therapist, Elliott learned to crawl for himself. I could see his face brighten with the feeling of power this gave him. He began crawling everywhere, investigating every room of Tillie and Julius' house. Every accessible drawer was yanked open, its contents spilled out and meticulously inspected. Rooms began to look as though they had been turned sideways, with every unsecured item swept to the carpet and scattered. It was wonderful.

Elliott learned to take Uncle Julius by the hand and every morning he lead him to the closet in our room. A low rod had been attached underneath my clothes for all of Elliott's apparel. Elliott would point out what he wanted to wear that day and Julius would help him get dressed.

The therapy also awakened other areas of activity in Elliott. He began making specific sounds that were not yet words, but which had definite meanings—for food, for the bathroom, for play, to go outside. Julius and Tillie were constantly patient and understanding, and they were always there to cater to the needs of my son.

Florida was different in those days. There was no annual migration of snowbirds coming to roost on the undeveloped beaches, and there had been, as yet, no mass exodus from Cuba. Instead, pristine Art Deco buildings mingled with red-tiled Mediterranean homes in a world of towering banyans, fruit-laden mango trees, and healthy palms. The pace was slow and intoxicating. We would sit in the yard on a tropical night in mid-winter, and it was hard to feel burdened with Elliott's problems. There was much love here, and my son was making progress.

"We'd like you to leave Elliott here," Julius said to me one night.

"What?" The comment startled me and I looked up into his serious face. Tillie was sitting close to him, leaning forward in eager anticipation.

It was obvious that they had been discussing this for quite some time, but I couldn't understand why.

"We want you to leave Elliott here with us. He's obviously making progress and…"

"Oh, Julius, thank you, but I couldn't leave him. And I do have to be getting back to Eddie soon. Who knows how long Elliott will need therapy?"

"It doesn't matter how long." Tillie spoke now, unable to contain herself any longer. "If he lives with us he will always be near his therapist, and here he can enjoy the sunshine all year. You see how he likes it. Rose, we can't have a boy of our own. If you let us, we can adopt him and really help him. You've got plenty of time for other children at your age. You could go home and have another."

I was startled. I sat back in my chair, uncertain how to reply. No one was going to take my son from me, no matter what his problem was.

Still, I could see the hope in their eyes. Tillie and Julius had been like parents to me, and I knew that the only shadow in Tillie's bright, good-natured world was the fact that she would always be childless. She sat in her chair, small, plump and earnest, and it was hard not to sympathize with her. Julius would be a good father as well. He was often mistaken for Barry Goldwater and had the same conservative, well-humored nature. He patted his wife's hand softly and tried to put things into more rational terms.

"It's for your sake as much as Elliott's," he said quietly. "Give us a chance, Rose. We could make such a good home for the boy. You've seen how we've helped so far."

I stood up, confused and embarrassed by their gesture. "I think I had better go inside now. It's getting late." I tried to start for the door, but I knew I couldn't leave the matter open. "I appreciate the offer, I really do. But Elliott's *my* son. He's my only child. We've come so far together. You must understand." I left them sitting on the porch and hurried inside.

The next morning I remained in my room longer than usual. Elliott was crawling about on the floor, repeatedly going over to the door and trying to open it. He was confused about being shut in and kept looking at me questioningly, but I had no idea how I was going to face Tillie and Julius again. I had explained my reasons, but I knew it had taken tremendous courage for them to even ask me; I hated to disappoint them after all they had done for us. Finally, I composed myself, opened the door, and followed Elliott as he scampered toward the kitchen.

Things never go as you expect. I turned the corner to the kitchen table, and much to my surprise, Eddie was standing there with a cup of coffee in his hand.

"Surprise!" he said, beaming.

Elliott held back a moment, confused, and then sped over to his father. Eddie laughed with delight and scooped his son into the air, grinning enthusiastically while Tillie and Julius looked on from the other side of the room.

"Look at you, Elliott! Crawling" My son is growing up."

I could hold back no longer. I rushed around the corner of the table and squeezed both of my men together.

"When did you get here, Eddie?"

"I arrived about twenty minutes ago," he said, letting Elliott slip down to the floor and go scooting away for his morning hug from Aunt Tillie. Eddie leaned over and kissed me on the lips.

"I missed you, Rose," he said softly.

"I missed you too, Eddie, but what are you doing here?"

"I drove down with a friend so we could spend a few days together before going home." He squeezed me. "We have to celebrate Elliott's progress."

From the safety of Eddie's arms, I saw the disappointment wash over Tillie's and Julius' faces. But it didn't matter. I had a family and I would keep it together. That had to be my priority.

We spent the next day introducing Eddie to the sights of Miami. Elliott, in particular, enjoyed the beach and a last chance to splash in the tepid ocean waters. However, despite its growing reputation as an elite resort, Miami Beach still lacked most of the commercialism and tourist attractions that crowd it today. Fortunately, we were able to get away alone and enjoy each other in a momentarily perfect world.

On our last night, we celebrated with a special dinner with Tillie and Julius. When we had finished eating, Tillie and I retired to the kitchen with the dishes. I knew exactly what was on her mind.

"You haven't reconsidered, have you, Rose?"

"Tillie, I'm sorry, but I can't leave Elliott behind."

"Please remember that we asked because you live up north, Rose. Your uncle and I want him very much. If you can't get anyone to help the boy any more, we'd like to adopt him legally if we could, but we don't mean to suggest that he shouldn't be with his mother." She stopped washing the dishes for a moment, looking like she was about to cry. "You're always welcome here," she said. "All three of you."

"I appreciate it, Tillie. Really. But Elliott needs us and we can help him now. He's getting better."

A gale of laughter burst through from the other room. Tillie and I rushed to the doorway to see what was going on. Elliott was kneeling on the bathroom threshold, triumphantly clutching one end of a roll of toilet tissue. The rest of the roll left a labyrinth trail behind him, snaking in and out of the bathtub, around the sink, into the hall, and up and down the hall walls. Elliott's eyes were wide open with pride at his accomplishment.

And I was proud of him, too!

Chapter 5

By the fall of 1940, Elliott was two years old and was still unable to stand erect, talk, or coordinate his leg muscles. He continued to have difficulty grasping and holding things, and was squirming and twisting as much as ever. I begged Eddie to let me see another doctor, the chief pediatrician at the Children's Hospital in Pittsburgh. After a lengthy discussion, he agreed.

We waited in the doctor's office while he examined Elliott. Then, while a nurse kept Elliott busy, the doctor came in and settled in his chair. We'd been through this routine with other doctors, but this time, the result was a bit clearer.

"Well, Mr. and Mrs. Weiss, I'll get right down to business," he said. "We know what's wrong with your child."

I felt my heart lurch and leaned forward in my chair.

"I'm afraid that Elliott is a spastic," the doctor told us. "It's a condition that results from brain damage early in life. The affliction manifests itself in a number of different ways, depending on the part of the brain that's been damaged."

"Damaged...but how?"

"Probably from the lack of oxygen for the first few moments when he was born. That's a terribly critical moment."

"But how can you be certain so quickly?" My remaining hopes that Elliott would prove to be normal after all were rudely disappearing from sight.

"We're as certain as we can be. Mrs. Weiss, I've been with the Children's Hospital for quite a number of years now. We see a lot of things that the normal general practitioner in a small town never encounters. We've had children just like Elliott brought to us for diagnosis when other doctors have failed to identify the problem, through no fault of their own. We are a highly-acclaimed teaching hospital. We have little doubt as to the nature of the affliction or to its cause. I'm sorry."

Eddie gave me a warning look, certain that I was about to burst into tears, but I was too stunned. I could only sit there, wringing my hands and listening to the doctor.

"What does this mean exactly?" Eddie asked him.

"Well, there are a number of characteristics of a spastic child. Sometimes their heads wiggle helplessly, sometimes they're rigid, sometimes they're overly mobile. Again, it depends on the nature of the damage to the brain."

"But will Elliott get well?" I asked.

"He'll always have a physical handicap to overcome, Mrs. Weiss. Damage to the brain doesn't go away. But I can venture a guess that he *will* be able to talk some day. However, most of these children don't develop the coordination to walk on their own."

"But what can my husband and I do to help him get better? There has to be something."

"You can take him home and feed him well. Try to keep him warm and comfortable and happy, Mrs. Weiss. And thank God for the blessings you *do* have."

"But what about school?"

The doctor's eyebrows arched and an edge of impatience crept into his voice. "School? No school would accept him, Mrs. Weiss. Even an institution is going to have too much difficulty caring for him properly. My best advice is for you to keep on as you've been doing."

"It's not right," I told Eddie, using a handkerchief to mop away the inevitable tears as we drove away from Pittsburgh. I held Elliott tightly in my lap, finally letting my anguish out.

"It's not right. Elliott has as much right to enjoy this world as anybody else. There has to be a way to save him from this kind of life."

"Rose," Eddie said carefully, "you've got to accept what the doctor told us. Together we have to care for Elliott the best way we can, but we can't build up our hopes too much. Just take things as they come and the Lord will give us the strength to do what we have to for Elliott. The Lord has a reason for making him this way, even if we can't see it right now. We just have to do the best we can."

The words were easy, but how does a mother come to terms with the fact that there is something definitely and permanently wrong with her son? I now had to face that fact, Lord's will or not.

First, you try to place the blame on someone else. Many excuses came to mind. Dr. Wilson must have given me too much medication at Elliott's birth or during the pregnancy itself. The prescriptions from the other doctors had harmed Elliott in some way. I had not been given proper consultations by my friends and parents during pregnancy, and something they had told me to do resulted in this thing that had happened to my boy. I wondered if the flu I had during the third month of pregnancy could have been a factor. I wondered lots of things, some more logical than others.

When none of these rationalizations worked, I blamed myself. Perhaps I had not eaten properly, or maybe the walks I had taken while I was pregnant had done him some harm. Could climbing the stairs day after day to our second floor apartment have caused him harm?

I went through the physical disabilities, then turned to the spiritual ones. You can really damn yourself with these thoughts! "What did I do to make God angry with me? Perhaps it was punishment for not keeping strictly to our religion, for not being as devout as Eddie. Perhaps we had married too young, when we were untested, and God thought we needed an obstacle to overcome together. Perhaps I had not been good enough to Eddie and this challenge was meant to bring us closer together."

My positive thoughts turned blacker after that. "Perhaps there's no God at all, or perhaps there is a God but He's vengeful. Maybe there was some evil in me that was expressing itself through my child."

Eddie's faith was an encouragement. Perhaps it was because he was always so quiet, but he seemed so strong in his faith. He was thirty-three now and I felt protected by his maturity. If he said that this was the Lord's doing and that things would work out, then I had to cling to that thought.

In Judaism, there are many stories about dealing with adversityCstories that teach you to laugh at your misfortunes because things could always be far worse. I remember one tale about a man in Poland who went to a *shadchen*, a professional matchmaker. The matchmaker introduced him to a beautiful girl and he took her for a stroll through the park in Gdansk. After taking the girl home, he turned quickly to the shadchen and said, AThis girl is beautiful, Mrs. Hinkel, but she has a terrible limp."

"Only when she walks," Mrs. Hinkel replied.

That's how I should think of Elliott," I told myself. He's so beautiful, such a perfect baby. He snuggled close in my arms as the car climbed the hills out of Pittsburgh, and no one could have told by looking at him that there was anything wrong.

There's another story about Mrs. Hinkel. Another suitor returned to her one evening, livid, while his Adate" sat just outside the door in their carriage. "You've swindled me," he hissed at her. "Never have I seen a creature as ugly as this one you've sent me out with. She's old, she's ugly as an old horse, she lisps, and she squints like a mole."

"There's no need to whisper," Mrs. Hinkel said. "She's deaf, too."

There was always that uneasiness, the chance that Elliott's disease would lead to further complications, or that there was something else wrong that we had not recognized yet.

Brain damage sounded so terrible, so final, so permanent. But people came back from strokes and learned to walk again. Wasn't a stroke a form of brain damage? People were injured in car accidents, or shot in the head in the war, and they survived and regained their faculties. Why should this disability with my son be so final? Why couldn't we find some way to overcome it?

I was in denial again, back where I had been long before the trip to Pittsburgh. At long last, here was a doctor who had experience with hundreds of these cases, yet he was telling me to go home and keep Elliott warm and comfortable and to expect no more progress for the rest of his life.

But how can you tell someone to live without hope? I wouldn't have the heart. I couldn't do it. And with that, the quest that would shape the rest of my life was well underway.

Even today, the medical facts seem inhuman and cruel in their analytical finality. Cerebral palsy strikes as the result of an injury to the brain at birth or shortly afterward. The disability has three major forms, depending on the location of the injury. What follows is what the doctor in Pittsburgh had tried to explain, facts which I could not comprehend in the midst of the terrible verdict:

The largest part of the brain is the cerebral cortex, the convoluted grayish tissue most of us think of when we speak of the brain. It is divided into four lobes of varying sizes: the frontal lobe, the parietal lobe, the temporal lobe, and the occipital lobe. The active nerve cells of the cortex, about eight billion of them, organize all the information that is fed into the brain from our various senses. If the injury occurs in this area of the brain, the result is the Aspastic" form of cerebral palsy.

A much smaller section of the brain, located under the cortex, is the cerebellum. The brain centers its control of coordination and balance in the cerebellum. An injury to this section of the brain is called ataxia.

The third type of this disability strikes the brain stem or basal ganglia. It is called athetoid palsy. In most cases, the disability combines all three types of damage.

For a long time people with the disability were called Aspastics" as a blanket reference, although the term, with all its cruel connotations, actually referred to only one form of the affliction. It has also been called Little's Disease, among many other much crueler names in the vernacular.

In spastic palsy, the victim's limbs move as a solid piece, making movement rigid and unnatural. If the victim ever learns to walk, he develops a scissors gait that makes the legs cross with every step. Speech is difficult and the mouth drools almost constantly, a side effect that causes most people to automatically assume the victim of the disease is mentally impaired.

In contrast to this rigidity, in athetosis the victim has mobile spasms with involuntary, slow wiggling movements. When he tries to move, he has a writhing motion and his face contorts into weird grimaces, again leading people to believe that he is incapable of normal intelligence. Athetosis can also manifest itself in another form, chorea, an involuntary and irregular jerkiness of motion which forces its victim to use a hopping gait.

Finally, there is ataxia. In many ways it is the worst of all the variations of cerebral palsy. This was Elliott's problem. Ataxia is a lack of balanced action between opposing muscle groups, with a consequent clumsiness of movement. The person with ataxia suffers from slurred speech, tremors, and a rolling or staggering gait like that of a drunken person. Muscles tend to be more flaccid than rigid. When the ataxic person tries to pick up something, he brings his arm down in a swoopCthe classic description is Alike an eagle on a rabbit." There is a disordered sense of position. The ataxic person is not always certain where his arms and legs are, or what they are doing. His mind is a parent to his limbs, which behave like a quartet of unruly children.

Each of the descriptions of the condition mentions what it is like for a person who is mobileChow the condition affects someone who is otherwise normal. I grasped that notion and then remembered something else. Approximately a year earlier there had been an article in *Reader's Digest* about a doctor in Florida with cerebral palsy who spoke about his own struggle to overcome the malady, and how he subsequently established a residential school to treat the disability. Although I had not applied the story to our own case when I first read the article, nor to the particular name of the demon that possessed Elliott, I later realized that the doctor was writing about the same condition that plagued Elliott. Now I knew the name of Elliott's condition, and I hoped that would help us to fight back.

When we arrived home, Elliott was asleep. While Eddie carried him upstairs, I went to the bookshelf to search through the back issues of my magazines for the article in *Reader's Digest*. I found the story quickly and reread it while Eddie was tucking Elliott into bed. He came out in a few minutes, stretched his arms to fight away the knots from the long drive, and sat down in his favorite chair.

"Rose, I'm sorry that it had to end like this, but I guess it's best to know just where we stand with this thing. We can still make Elliott a good home and be as much a family as possible, but now we know there's not much else for us beyond that."

"Eddie, I want to go to Florida again."

He tilted his head to the side, clearly surprised at the conversation's new direction.

"Florida? I don't know if we can really afford another trip to see Tillie and Julius right now, Rose. I know they were good to you and Elliott and all but..."

"Eddie, there's another doctor."

There was a long moment of silence as Eddie stared at me, and I felt my resolve coming away at the edges. But I held on, and when Eddie didn't respond immediately, I plunged ahead.

"His name is Dr. Earl R. Carlson, and he's got the same things wrong with him that are wrong with Elliott. He couldn't control his muscles either. He couldn't speak. He was spastic— just like Elliott—and he beat it. He still struggles with his walking and with his speech, but now he's got a clinic in Florida and he's teaching other children."

"Rose, you heard what the doctor said today."

"Yes, but he never had to face the problem himself. Here's a man, just like Elliott, who says that with intensive training, concentration, and therapy, this thing can be beaten. The doctor beat this thing and now his patients are doing it. Eddie, this means there is hope as long as we act while Elliott's young enough to learn."

Eddie lowered his head, and I could see him weighing the alternatives.

"I don't know, Rose. You have to think about this too. I don't know if I want you away from me that long. On the other hand, if you look into this school and you're convinced it looks like it might be good for Elliott, then I can't say no to you."

I wrote to Dr. Carlson, explaining in detail the diagnosis from Children's Hospital and our own observations of our son. As I wrote, the hopes built up inside me again.

But what if this man couldn't help Elliott either? What if he wouldn't see him? What if he wouldn't accept him into his program? What if it was more than we could afford? There was no one else to turn to, no one else who understood.

In spite of himself, I could see that Eddie was building up his expectations as well. He had read Dr. Carlson's article along with excerpts from his life story, *Born That Way*, which has become the classic text on the development cerebral palsy victims. Dr. Carlson had overcome severe physical handicaps to become a pediatrician so that he could treat others, who, like himself, were Aborn that way." That was Dr. Carlson's expression for children born with cerebral palsy, and he used that expression for the title of his own life story, *Born That Way*.

Dr. Carlson's book tells about his personal struggle for physical strength and emotional maturity in his attempt to make a place for himself in the world. Not surprisingly, Eddie and I saw much promise in Dr. Carlson's words. When I told Eddie about my fears he would say, AWe'll worry when the time comes, Rose. Don't borrow trouble right now. If Dr. Carlson can't take Elliott, maybe there will still be a way. Maybe we don't have to abandon all hope after all."

Eddie also was hoping again. And so was I.

Chapter 6

After two weeks that passed like years, we finally received a letter inviting us to bring Elliott to Pompano Beach, Florida for an examination by Dr. Carlson. By this time, Elliott, who was now almost four years old, had stopped improving at home. His awkward crawl remained the same and he still couldn't balance himself well enough to stand up. Walking, of course, was impossible for him.

As for his speech, Elliott was trying to learn new words, although his only recognizable words were Ama-ma" and Ada-da." I spent every spare moment trying to expand his tiny vocabulary, pointing out things around him, patiently reciting their names and then searching for a coherent reply. "Ta-ble," "win-dow," "pup-py." Elliott seemed interested, staring at the place where I pointed and listening carefully at the name I gave the object. When it was something he liked, he would show obvious delight. And he was equally definite in things that he disliked. The words, however, were beyond his power. Awkward bodily gestures and contorted facial expressions continued to be his primary means of communication.

The Carlson School at Pompano Beach housed about 60 residents, ranging in age from 3 years old to adult, most of them quite severely handicapped. The majority of the residents came from wealthy homes. In the economy of 1940, the $160 monthly tuition was, as you can imagine, a tremendous sum for Eddie and me to pay, but we were ready to sacrifice whatever was necessary to give our son the chance in life he deserved.

Dr. Carlson explained that many children made excellent progress within a year's time at his school, progress which enabled many of them to return to a relatively Anormal" life. He conceded too, that some would remain with him for years. Admittedly, I was cautious, but what choices did Eddie and I have?

As for Dr. Earl Carlson himself, his mother had saved him. She died when he was only 20, but during the years she was with him she refused to give up hope. When he fought her, she fought him harder. When he wanted to give up, she persevered. When he fell, she picked him up; when he was weak, she was strong. She made him walk and talk and learn, and in the end she made him more than a manCshe made him great. Eddie and I could do no less for our son.

Years earlier, Dr. Carlson had fallen ill, and had called in a German nurse to take care of him. She had been gentle, patient, and loving. Before long, he regained his strength, married her, and together they founded a school for brain-damaged children on Long Island. Over the years it expanded from the nursery school level through high school, and then they opened a second facility in Florida. Now the residents of the school alternated between the facilities, spending the warm summers on the beaches of Long Island and the winters in the healthy Florida sun.

As I sat patiently, waiting through another interminable examination for Dr. Carlson's decision, I watched him work and drew strength from his own victory over the disease. He was a slightly built man with intense eyes and sallow features. Only the awkward position of his hands and the rolling manner in which he walked gave a clue to the deformity he constantly battled.

It was painful hearing Dr. Carlson diagnose Elliott as an "ataxia" type of spastic, but he ended his evaluation with the words that I had come to Florida to hear. "There's a chance that Elliott will eventually be able to walk. He could learn to talk, and someday he might very well attend normal schools, even college, if he so desires. Consequently, Mrs. Weiss, I'm pleased to tell you that we can accept Elliott for our nursery program."

I was ecstatic. At that instant, and all of my doubts vanished. Whatever the cost, Eddie and I would scrape it together; whatever the burden, we would share it. The loss of our precious child's company at home, not seeing his beautiful smile, not feeling the warmth of his loving arms, as dear as these tender moments are to young parents with their first child, all seemed a small price to pay for the chance that Elliott could learn to walk and talk and mature into a normal young man.

"I imagine this will mean some hardship on your part," Dr. Carlson said.

"I understand," I agreed. "I don't want to give up Elliott, not if you can do something for him…" I was willing to sacrifice anything, even if it meant a painful separation from my beloved son.

"I think we can do a great deal for him. We're not like most institutions which deal with the handicapped. Our purpose goes beyond keeping the children occupied. We attempt to give them all of the education they are capable of absorbing, and all of the physical ability that is possible for them. We have to develop their concentration, perseverance, and ability if they are ever to overcome their handicap and adjust to their environment as contributing members of society.

"And when I speak of hardship for you, I don't necessarily mean the hardship of separation, or of the somewhat considerable cost of maintaining Elliott in this program. I mean that you must, in your own contacts with Elliott, maintain the same strict regimen that he will face here.

"From my own experience, and from the things that I have seen here, I know that many parents and teachers make too many concessions to the handicapped. This is unfair to them because if we make things too easy, these children never develop the ability to fight their affliction. Instead, the spastic may develop behavioral dysfunctions that make it difficult, if not impossible, to conform to normal standards. And that, of course, is our ultimate goal, to make your son as normal as possible.

"While he is here, he will be subjected to rigid discipline and strict routine. These methods result in much more rapid improvement than leniency and compassion.

My entire body went weak at the words. I had to bring my handkerchief from my purse and dab my eyes before I could reply. "Doctor, let's whatever it takes. I don't know how to thank you enough."

He waited patiently while I composed myself and then continued.

"It won't be easy, Mrs. Weiss, but I think Elliott has come to us in time. Early treatment of this problem is essential. Even now, he must unlearn the motion habits he has developed. He must be taught to use his body correctly. With ataxia, this is a particularly difficult problem because the individual does not always have a clear idea of what his limbs are doing. There seems to be a gap in the path that the brain uses to get messages to and from the arms and legs. We have to develop new pathways for these messages to travel.

"We also need to begin immediate work on his personality development. At his age, he is already developing the character traits that will individualize him throughout his life. Unless these traits are carefully shaped through discipline and reward, the spastic individual may easily become neurotic or even psychotic. We must make certain that this does not happen to your son."

Dr. Carlson leaned forward across his desk, engrossed in what he was saying, although he must have lectured a thousand mothers in the same manner over the years. I could hear the conviction ringing in his voice and I concentrated to absorb everything he was telling me.

"The greatest barrier to the treatment of children with cerebral palsy is the lack of self-discipline. They develop highly fluctuating emotions, from extreme depression to euphoria. When we examined Elliott today, he was in an excitable state. We expected this because the surroundings are unfamiliar to him. We have to gain his confidence before he can progress."

"Many times, when I see our children feeding and dressing themselves or learning to walk on crutches, I can't help thinking about the state they were in when their parents brought them to see me for the first time. We have to tame their excitability, for they can only progress in a calm, quiet atmosphere."

"What we will be doing for the next few weeks is getting Elliott to work with our therapists. They have all been carefully chosen for their ability to work with handicapped children. Too often, when a parent tries to teach a child to walk or talk, he or she may show too much anxiety over the child's progress, and the child becomes excitable and unmanageable as a reflection of this anxiety. Discipline is the answer. We will get him to relax, we will get him to concentrate, and then, Mrs. Weiss, we will get him to walk."

"Just tell me what to do."

He smiled with satisfaction and stood up, and again I marveled at his mobility and vigor in spite of his handicap.

"Right now, all I need you to do is go home and try not to worry. We'll take care of your son. If you like, I can have one of the attendants show you around the school before you leave. I think you will understand that your son will be in a very positive environment."

The Carlson School was, indeed, beautiful. It was situated on a beautiful section of rambling beachfront property that might have been mistaken for a luxurious tourist hotel. The building was of the typical Mediterranean style that had become popular in South Florida. It had a red barrel-tiled roof and arched doorways hinting of Moorish origins. On the eastern side of the building, a white strand of beach was bordered by palm trees and seagrape trees stretching for miles in either direction, all of this in an area once reserved for millionaire vacationers.

Inside were spacious hallways with high ceilings and beautiful chandeliers. The severely handicapped children were housed in ground floor rooms while the others lived upstairs. Areas for speech, occupational and physical therapy, as well as formal schoolrooms were held in what obviously had been the drawing rooms and parlors of a magnificent estate.

There were about 60 residents at the school at that time. Most of them were even more severely handicapped than Elliott. I didn't question this, or the fact that the school was located between the two most prestigious East Coast resorts of the era. It was symbolic of Dr. Carlson's personal success, and I would only have the best for my child. In 1940, the $160 monthly tuition was an overwhelming sum, but Elliott needed a chance in life, and, if we had to, we would buy it for him.

"Ideally, we would like to keep Elliott for a year," Dr. Carlson said as he saw me out. "After that, as I've explained, there's a good chance he'll be ready to go home and take up a relatively normal existence. In some cases, however, we need to keep the child longer, sometimes for a lifetime. All I can promise is that we'll do what's best for Elliott."

During this conversation, Elliott was waiting with the attendants by the door. I knelt beside him, my hands cold and sweaty and my legs trembling. He smiled at me and he hugged me tightly with his feeble arms. I was barely able to find my voice. I think he knew that I was going to be leaving without him.

"Goodbye, Elliott. Be a good boy for the nice people here."

I held him tightly, refusing to let go until one of the attendants gently touched my shoulder. I drew back slowly and they took Elliott away, pushing him down the hallway in his stroller. And then he was gone.

I left the school, but I was reluctant to go too far. Tillie and Julius were, as always, open in their hospitality, and I decided to remain in Florida so that I could visit Elliott. During the next few weeks, I visited the school frequently. Elliott seemed happy and well cared for, and he was adjusting rapidly. He was, in fact, making his first friends. He had never had true companionship, but here, with others similarly afflicted, he could be treated as an equal and communicate with children his own age. What we found even more encouraging in the first few weeks was that Elliott had begun to utter clear syllables and was beginning to string them together into coherent words.

Elliott's progress seemed miraculous, but when I returned home with Tillie and Julius, there was a great void in the household. I missed my son.

"I wouldn't worry, Rose," Tillie told me. "Eddie needs you back home, and Elliott has us here to look after him. We'll visit him every Sunday and take him on rides, buy him ice cream, show him he's still loved. Things couldn't be better."

She couldn't hide the eagerness in her voice. She was getting Elliott after all. I couldn't resent them for loving my son, but the situation was disconcerting nonetheless. Tillie would be a part-time parent by proxy and I would be returning home alone.

Elliott couldn't have more loving parents than Eddie and myself. How could I travel a thousand miles away and leave him there? It just didn't seem right.

"Think of Eddie, home alone," Julius offered. "You know he married you for your cooking, Rose. The poor man is probably wasting away on canned food."

That, at least, brought a smile to my face. It was true. Eddie hated to cook and he hated going out to restaurants. I was neglecting him, but he had managed for 30 years before he'd gotten his live-in chef. Elliott had never been alone before.

"At least he'll be coming up to Long Island this summer," I rationalized. "That's not too far to visit."

"Of course not," Julius said beaming. "You can come see us next winter."

And so I left them and my son and went back to the cold North. Eddie was delighted with my return.

But without Elliott the house seemed empty. Each time I passed his room with the new bed and matching chest of drawers, each time I looked at the colorful hooked rug with the dog in the center, a rug I had made especially for Elliott's room, tears came to my eyes. I cried a lot during the next few months, tears that only a mother's heart can know. But I found solace and strength in telling myself that this was the only way my child could be helped.

Aunt Tillie and Uncle Julius visited Elliott faithfully each Sunday afternoon while he was in Pompano Beach. They wrote often, describing how Elliott anxiously awaited them, not budging from the lobby sofa until they arrived.

Every Sunday meant love and affection for Elliott: hugs, kisses, a ride in the car, and a not-to-be-missed ice cream treat. They sent us many pictures showing Elliott's developing maturity.

One day the school informed me that a local carpenter had constructed a large wooden walker for Elliott. "It's sort of box-shaped, rectangular, and has bars on each side," the letter said. "Elliott is using the walker to give him support, and he pushes it along the sidewalks to make his daily rounds of the school." Pictures of Elliott and the walker were enclosed in the letter. We also learned that if he couldn't make it go fast enough to suit him, he would simply crawl out of it and scamper about on his hands and knees.

"In no time he'll be able to take care of himself, and you and I can get on with our life together," Eddie assured me.

"But what kind of life is it if we have to abandon Elliott?"

"We haven't abandoned him, Rose. It's just for a little while."

But I couldn't cast away the doubts. Instead I found myself pacing the living room floor, wringing my hands, wondering how Elliott was doing. The letters from the school were encouraging, but I wondered how much they were self-serving and how much they really reflected Elliott's contentment.

Eddie returned from the pharmacy one night to find me standing in the nursery, staring at Elliott's things, fighting tears for the thousandth time. He put his arm around me.

"I thought we might go out to dinner tonight. You can use a night away from the dishes."

"I had to use the house money for the rent, Eddie," I told him. "There's a casserole in the oven."

"In that case a casserole will be fine. We can go for a nice walk after dinner."

"I don't feel like walking, Eddie." I took a last look around Elliott's bedroom and then went into the kitchen to sit down at the table. Eddie followed me.

"Rose, you're going to have to snap out of it. You can't have Elliott and help him at the same time. We're doing what's best for him."

"It's not fair, Eddie. It's not what I wanted our life to be like."

The tears were gushing now, and I put my head in my hands to hide them while my back was racked with sobs. Eddie watched for a moment, and I could sense his body tensing without having to look at him.

"Rose, we can't go on like—" he started, and then stopped so sharply I looked up at him. He was clutching his stomach with a look of disgust on his face. He whirled away from me and hurried into the bathroom. Alarmed, I ran after him and got there just in time to see him pour a spoonful of his medicine from the cabinet and swallow it.

"Eddie, are you all right?"

He capped the bottle, not looking at me.

"Elliott's going to be all right, Rose. We're going to keep on doing for him like we've been doing. We'll go to the bank tomorrow and get a loan so we can afford to get by for now."

"Eddie, we don't need a loan. We can find other ways to save. I'm shopping the bargains now, and I stay out of the department stores so I won't buy anything. We can skip the dinners and the movies, and we really don't need any more clothes. Maybe we can save enough to go see Elliott…"

Eddie was staring at me. He took a deep breath and then nodded.

"I'll try keeping the store open until nine, Rose. Maybe it will help. You can't deny yourself everything for Elliott's sake."

"But I will, Eddie, especially if it means I can see him."

He hugged me. "Rose, you love him so much."

I squeezed him back, grateful that he understood. When we finally separated, he tapped me on the chin affectionately.

"Are you sure you don't want to go for a walk with me tonight?"

"Maybe later," I said. "I'm putting together a care package and a letter for Elliott. When that's done, I'll walk with you if there's still time."

"Sure, Rose," he said. "I understand. We'll walk when you get that done."

By the time I was done with my letter and had sealed the box I was sending to Florida, I was ready for a short walk, but by that time, Eddie had got to bed and had fallen asleep.

Chapter 7

Elliott liked the Carlson School. His bed was along the wall of his room and there was a window above it where he could look out and see the birds. There were seagulls and pelicans and mockingbirds. He had a net, like a hammock, that was strung the length of the bed, and he had all his stuff in itChis clothes and books and everything. But he dreaded some of the things they made him do at the school. The staff was very tough on him, except for one. Ed Wobloscky was becoming a second father to Elliott. He was wonderful. Ed would take a horse cart and they would ride up and down the beach. They had a great time together.

"Elliott is so precious," Tillie wrote. "He knows that Sunday is the day we go to see him, and I don't know what he would ever do if we were forced to miss a trip. When we arrive, he is always sitting on the sofa in the lobby waiting for us. They've told us that sometimes he has waited almost an hour, but he won't budge if he knows we're coming.

"He's so much better than the other children at the school, Rose. Some of them are so pitiful, hardly able to do anything for themselves. But then there are many others who get around on crutches, or with braces, or sometimes without any help at all. I'm sure that's the way it will be with Elliott.

"He loves our visits because he knows they mean hugs and kisses and affection. He needs that after the routine of the school. He can't wait to get in the car for his Sunday drive. We take him to an ice cream parlor by the beach and he always has a big sundae. The people in the parlor know him now and are always very nice to him. It's so wonderful, Rose. I hope you're not worrying about him, because he really is in good hands."

That year, Dr. Carlson engaged a special train to take the children from Florida to East Hampton so they could travel in private—away from the cruel stares of other children and adults. He had established his Long Island school in an old estate similar to the one in Pompano Beach. It stood on a wooded site next to the breeze swept dunes of the southern coastal beach, where students could continue exercising in the ocean and enjoy the open air.

"Elliott is beginning to pronounce many words," the school told me. "He is making sentences and we can understand them. His coordination is much improved. In occupational therapy, he is learning to string wooden beads and to work with the pegboard. This helps him develop eye-hand coordination by requiring him to place square pegs in square holes, etc. While this is a simple task for a "normal" child, it is a significant accomplishment for Elliott."

"The children swim daily, weather permitting, and always under strict supervision. Elliott seems to be very happy with his surroundings; he is cooperative and his personality continues to be bright and cheerful, as you will see from the enclosed photographs."

The picture showed him playing on the beach with the other children and moving about the sidewalks in his walker. He was smiling in each picture. His legs seemed longer, and he was a great deal leaner. He looked like a beautiful young man, and from the pictures it was difficult to tell that he had any problems.

"Elliott's third birthday was a special event," another letter informed us. "We had a party for him on September 8th, complete with a chocolate cake and six candles—three for good luck."

"In addition, as you will see in the attached photo, Elliott has had his first professional haircut. We think you will agree he looks very handsome." My boy's baby curls were gone, replaced by an attractive crewcut. He looked like any other youngster ready to try out for Little League.

In physical therapy, Elliott was taking special daily sessions along parallel bars designed to help him develop greater control of his leg muscles. He wore high brown shoes for extra support, and he was learning how to lace and tie them. We purchased special clothing for him—pullover shirts, and trousers and underwear with elastic waistbands. In what seemed like no time at all, he was learning to dress himself.

"This is all very encouraging," said a letter from the school. "While we realize the development he has shown has taken some time, we feel that Elliott can continue to progress. We are returning to Pompano Beach shortly, and we hope you will permit us to keep Elliott with us for at least another year. We believe we can have him walking by then."

I found the letter opened on the table when I came home from visiting friends at midday. I read it with a sinking feeling, knowing that they wanted to keep me apart from my son for another year. The time had already seemed so long, and after all, how much of his progress could have been accomplished at home, surrounded by the love and affection of his family?

I wondered why Eddie had happened to be home before noon to open the letter. I looked around the living room curiously and then went to the bedroom door. Eddie was undressed and lying under the covers asleep. Alarmed, I hurried over to his side and rashly awakened him.

"Eddie, what's wrong?"

He shook off his sleep slowly, and when he looked at me he seemed weaker than I'd ever seen him.

"I didn't feel well, Rose. I had to come home." His voice was barely a whisper.

"Do you want me to call Dr. Wilson? Who's taking care of the store?"

"I already saw him. He told me to close up the store and come home to lie down."

"What's wrong? Is it the flu? Should I get you some chicken soup?"

"I couldn't keep down breakfast again," he said.

"Again?"

"I've been feeling weak and my stomach has been cramping on me. Dr. Wilson wants to run some tests, but he thinks it's a duodenal ulcer. He gave me some more medicine."

"He *thinks*? Eddie, you know how he was with Elliott. Maybe we should take you somewhere else to get checked. We can't afford to mess around with this. Maybe it's something serious."

"Rose, this time he's right." Eddie tried to make his voice stronger, and just barely succeeded. "And an ulcer *is* serious. He says if I keep on with this pressure, my condition will only get worse. He thinks that it might be a good idea if we didn't keep the store."

I sat down on the chair beside the bed.

"Eddie, what would we do? How will we afford to live?"

"We'd find a way to make do. Did you see the letter from Elliott's school?"

"Eddie, how can we keep him in school another year if you can't work?"

"I was thinking about it before you came home, Rose. What I really need is time to relax. The climate is bad for me here. Maybe we should both go to Florida for a while."

My feelings of impending tragedy immediately disappeared.

"Eddie, that would be perfect! We could stay with Tillie and Julius until you got better. Maybe you could open a store down there."

"Maybe we could. I'd have to pass the Florida pharmaceutical boards first, but they can't be any tougher than the ones here. Besides, I know a thing or two more about mixing potions than the kids coming fresh out of the University of Florida. I'd enjoy being close to Elliott down there and I know you'd feel better if you could see him more often."

"Oh, Eddie, let's do it!" I said. "I'll write Tillie and Julius right away. Do you think it will take long to sell the store?"

"The people from a chain in Pittsburgh have been wanting to get hold of it. I think we can make a deal that will keep us going for a while."

I was thrilled about the possibility of moving to Florida, but I was worried about Eddie's health. The strain of putting up a strong front for me had been wearing away at him. All this time he had been worried about Elliott, about me, about the store, and about paying our bills. And he had been trying to be so strong.

It would be better now. It really would. I could see Elliott whenever I wanted. He would know that I was still there for him and that I still loved him.

Much to my surprise, however, Tillie's reply to my letter seemed strangely formal:

"Dear Rose, of course we will be happy to have you and Eddie stay with us until you establish yourselves here. We will make up the spare bedroom again. Julius and I will be glad to accompany you whenever you wish to visit Elliott in Pompano. Sincerely, Aunt Tillie."

"That's an awfully short letter for your aunt," Eddie said. "Are you sure she doesn't think we're imposing?"

"No, not Tillie. She wouldn't dream of having us stay anywhere else. I think she's a little disappointed that she won't have Elliott to herself this year."

I felt triumphant when I said it, in spite of myself. Elliott had to know who his mother was. If he was going to succeed, and mature, I wanted to be a major part of it.

As Eddie predicted, the Pittsburgh company was eager to get the store and we made a good settlement for it. I soon found myself packing up our belongings and making preparations to leave the house where we had stayed since the day we were marriedCthe house where Elliott was born.

I waited on the sidewalk while Eddie closed up the store for the last time and handed the keys to one of the men from Pittsburgh. They shook hands, both of them smiling and laughing, but when Eddie walked away he looked pale. He stopped on the curb and took a last, long look at the front door of his business.

"It'll be all right," I told him, squeezing his arm.

He nodded, silent, and opened the car door for me. He paused another moment before walking around to the driver's seat, and when he slid behind the wheel he took a long, deep breath.

"You're not feeling ill, are you, Eddie?" I asked him.

He turned the key in the ignition and put the car in gear, but he waited before driving away. Eddie seemed to need a final look at his store before answering. "I'm just a little tired, Rose," he said softly.

That night, Eddie went to bed early, but he slept fitfully. Then he was up by 4:30 a.m., checking the house a final time for any forgotten items, and then he carefully stowed all our worldly goods into the car and trailer. I heard him moving about and got up to put on the coffee while he was taking a load of cartons downstairs, but the coffee pot and the coffee were already gone. I stood helplessly in my housecoat in the middle of the kitchen, wondering how I could prepare his breakfast so that he would have the strength for the drive. When he came in he knew immediately what I was thinking.

"We'll stop on the highway," he said. "It's good to have an early start."

I got dressed quickly and packed my housecoat into the suitcase. The closets were emptied, and the house looked as deserted as it had felt in the long months of my son's absence. We stopped at the threshold on the way out and I looked around, trying to engrave the last view of it in my mind.

"It's good to leave," Eddie said. "There has been so much sadness and worry here."

"But there were good times, too, Eddie. Lots of them."

"We'll have plenty more," he said, and he escorted me out the door to the car. The sun was coming up through the full leaves of the oak trees in the yard as we pulled out of the driveway and turned south. I told myself I wasn't going to look back, but I looked out the back window anyway until I could no longer see our home. I felt as if I was leaving part of my soul there, abandoned.

We drove down through the mountains to Cumberland and then followed the narrow Blue Ridge Highway south. In those days, interstate travel was a series of narrow roads and endless small towns. We had the usual tourist trepidations as we crossed the Mason-Dixon Line into Dixie, where every Northerner still imagined lingering Confederate provincialism and bigotry.

"Don't drive too fast, Eddie," I cautioned. "They'll see the Pennsylvania license plate and give you a ticket if you're not careful."

"I'm careful, Rose," he said. "I've done this before, you know?"

"I just want you to be careful, that's all."

Eddie laughed at me, and then we enjoyed the scenery for the first few hundred miles. As the strain of the drive began to wear on him, however, he talked less frequently. I could see his jaw set and his body become more rigid as he held the wheel. I wished that I had learned to drive so that I could relieve him for part of the journey. But there had never been much need for me to drive.

I dozed occasionally when the monotony of the journey began to wear on me. During the first day's travel, Eddie indulged me by stopping to let me look at scenery and small roadside attractions, but by the afternoon of the second day, he even wanted to avoid the rest stops. "Let's just get there already," he kept saying.

At night, in the motels, he tossed in his sleep, and I could hear him muttering wordless sentences in his dreams. He would get up several times during the night and head into the bathroom, where he would stay for a long time.

The temperature grew increasingly warm as we headed south. Our car was not air conditioned, and I could see the heat was starting to take its toll on Eddie. Sweat beaded on his forehead, and his face was becoming paler and paler. Now Eddie scarcely spoke to me at all, and he looked increasingly impatient when I said anything. But I could hardly keep still as I grew more and more excited with every mile we traveled closer to our destination.

"I'm sure the school will let me bring Elliott home now and then for vacations," I said. "We can take him to the beach again, Eddie. When we get a house, let's make sure that it's close to the beach. I like Coral Gables, if we can afford it. There are lots of nice old houses there that shouldn't cost very much. I was thinking about a duplex. We could live in one side and rent the other, using the rent money to pay off the mortgage. That way it would hardly cost anything. If you like, when we get there..."

And then I realized that the car was slowing down. Eddie pulled off to the side, very slowly, and when we came to a complete stop, he closed his eyes and leaned his head against the steering wheel.

"Eddie, what is it?"

"I just need a minute to rest, Rose. Just be quiet a minute."

Eddie was taking long, deep breaths, each one getting longer. Suddenly, he flung open the door, scrambled behind the car, and began retching violently onto the sandy shoulder. I rushed to help support him. At first he tried to wave me off, but as a new wave of nausea overcame him he clutched tightly to my support.

"Eddie..."But he had the dry heaves and couldn't answer. I looked around, frightened. A brownish-yellow plain surrounded us on all sides, broken only by scrub palmetto, pine trees, and cattle. The highway was an empty expanse of asphalt stretching interminably into the distance.

"Eddie, please, what can I do?"

He finally caught his breath and I helped him lean against the car. His skin was strangely cold, yet damp to the touch. Perspiration darkened his entire shirt.

"I'll be all right, Rose," he swore. "Just a little car sick."

"Eddie, you were never car sick when you were driving. You need to see a doctor."

"I'll see one in Miami, Rose. We'll make it. Just let me rest a while."

Against my better judgment, I let him go to sleep in the car. It was close to noon and the heat was becoming unbearable. I was certain that whatever was wrong with Eddie, sleeping in that oven wasn't going to help him. I rolled down all the windows and opened the doors on the passenger's side to let in as much breeze as possible, and then I stood outside the car, frantic, wondering what to do next. Every time a car passed, I wondered if I should stop it and ask them to send for help. Three cars finally did stop, but each time I wavered, sure that Eddie would be angry with me if I did anything. I assured them that everything was all right and sent them on their way.

I kept checking to make certain Eddie was breathing all right. His skin seemed to be burning, but I told myself that it was just the heat of the car's interior. Finally, about three o'clock in the afternoon, he woke up and sat upright behind the steering wheel. I looked at him with trepidation.

"Let's get started," he said, turning on the ignition.

"Eddie, let's stop somewhere close by. It's not too late to have someone look at you today."

He wasn't listening. He pulled onto the highway with exaggerated slowness.

"It's OK now. I'm rested. Let's just get there."

It was four more hours before we pulled up in front of the house in Miami. Julius and Tillie came out laughing and smiling, with arms spread to greet us, but their faces quickly took on a look of concern when they saw Eddie's condition.

He could barely walk. Julius quickly put an arm around him and helped him toward the house. Halfway to the door, Eddie's legs buckled and he nearly fell down. Julius regained his balance and guided Eddie through the front door.

"Rose, how could you let him drive like that?" Tillie demanded. "What's wrong with him?"

"I don't know," I said, hurrying after my husband. "We have to find a doctor for him. Tillie, I'm scared."

Chapter 8

"Tillie, I really appreciate your offer to let us stay with you and Julius again, but I think it would be better if we rented a room closer to the hospital. Eddie is seeing so many doctors and the traveling back and forth is not good for him."

"I understand, Rose, but if you should change your mind, both of you are more than welcome to stay with us," Tillie replied.

"Mr. Weiss, I'm, sorry to say this, but the tests show you have an ulcer and your appendix is on the verge of perforating. The only cure is surgery as quickly as possible," said Dr. Hanson.

"Doctor, he will be all right, won't he?" I said, searching for assurance.

"Yes, Mrs. Weiss, he'll be fine. Your husband will be in the intensive care unit for a few days and then in a regular ward for about ten days. After that, he can go home."

Eddie's surgery lasted about two hours, although it felt like two years. Finally, the doctor came out to see me.

"Mrs. Weiss, your husband is in the recovery room and doing well," the doctor told me.

After fourteen days in the hospital, Eddie came home and I gave him all the loving care I could to get him back onto his feet. Once he started to feel better, he began to study for the Florida Pharmaceutical Examination. I knew he was worried about something, but he had been a pharmacist for a long time, so I knew it wasn't about the exam.

"Eddie, what's wrong?" I asked. "You seem preoccupied about something and it can't be the exam, because I know you'll have no problems there," I said one evening.

"We've spent just about all of our savings from the sale of the pharmacy and I haven't been able to buy another one here in Miami Beach. What are we going to do when the money runs out?"

"Eddie, I've been worried about the money too, but we've always done okay and I'm sure that in the future we'll be just fine. All you have to do is pass the examination and then you can focus more attention on starting up your own business here."

Two weeks later we were on our way to Gainesville. Eddie passed his examination without any problems, but instead of going back to Miami, he suggested we head back to Pennsylvania for a while.

I wasn't happy about this decision, especially given what we'd gone through leaving California, PA and moving to Florida, but he'd been so ill; he needed me and I couldn't say no to him.

After a couple of weeks in Pennsylvania, Eddie came home happier than I'd seen him in a long time.

"Rose, I found a pharmacy for sale here in town that we can afford. I want to buy it so that we can get back on our feet again," he said.

I had hoped that this stay in Pennsylvania would be short-lived and that we would soon go back to Elliott, but once again I couldn't say no. Eddie was so positive and happy.

February of 1942 marked Elliott's second full year with Dr. Carlson. That month we received a letter from the school suggesting we take Elliott home and enroll him in a kindergarten for normal youngsters in preparation for entrance into public school.

Progress had been slow. Elliott could dress himself and he seemed to have better control of his muscles, but he still could not walk independently. Nevertheless, Dr. Carlson believed he should be home with us and exposed to normal children for emotional reasons.

The letter, combined with the numbing cold of the Pennsylvania winters, and with my loneliness, would help us make a decision.

"Eddie," I shouted as I rushed into the store, "Elliott can come home and we can be a family again."

Eddie's face showed relief. Finally, his son was making progress, and maybe soon we would be a normal family.

"There's a problem though, Eddie," I said.

"What now, Rose," he replied.

"It will soon be winter here and Elliott is not used to the cold and damp anymore. I think I should go back to Florida and get a house down there. You could visit us and see the progress he is making."

I could see from the look on Eddie's face that he was not happy with this idea.

"Eddie, we've come so far with Elliott," I said. "Why destroy all of his progress now?"

"OK, Rose, you go to Florida and I'll stay here and keep the business going. I'll visit you when I can," he said resignedly.

Once again, I found myself back on the train to Florida. This time, my son would be back home with me. When I arrived, I rented a unit in a small duplex, brought Elliott home from Dr. Carlson's, and called Sarah, the nurse who had been with me at his birth.

"Sarah," I said. "Elliott is home and I will need some help taking care of him. Can you come and stay with me? I'll pay you fifteen dollars a week plus room and board."

"I'll be there in a couple of hours," she said. "I'd love to help you with Elliott." Sarah also agreed to go to Dr. Carlson's with me to observe the therapy treatments so that we would know how to continue them on our own. However, I didn't know how soon Sarah's generosity would end.

"Elliott, you're going to school today," I told him. "You will be with other little boys and girls your age. Isn't that exciting?"

He laughed with delight. At least now, maybe, he would have friends.

But when I took Elliott to the school the principal said, AI'm sorry, Mrs. Weiss, but Elliott's attention span does not allow him to do the things the other children are doing and he gets very disruptive. I'm very sorry," he added.

"Don't worry, Mrs. Weiss," Sarah said. "Maybe if I stay at the school with him, he'll be better."

"That's a good idea, Sarah. I'm sure they won't mind you being there to help."

Once again, I heard the same story from the principal. The only time Elliott behaved in class was when Sarah was with him. Otherwise, he distracted the other children. And when it came time for the children's rest period, he wouldn't leave them alone. I noticed he was becoming more and more emotionally disturbed. I was sure that Elliott was acting out his frustrations over not being able to do the things the other children were doing.

I tried one more time at a different kindergarten, with Sarah taking care of Elliott at the school which was run by two middle-aged ladies who liked Sarah.

"I'm sorry, Mrs. Weiss," Sarah said one day, "but they have offered me one hundred dollars a week to go work for them full-time."

"Please, Sarah, stay and help me with Elliott," I pleaded. "You know how fond he is of you. You can do so much with him."

I decided now was time to purchase a small pair of adjustable wooden crutches. Each afternoon Sarah and I spent time with Elliott in the front yard trying to get him to take a few steps. Although the crutches had foam-rubber pads, he complained of pain constantly. "They hurt me here," he said, pointing under his arms in defiance of the crutches and, perhaps, of the world.

He tried again to take one step, then flung the crutches in the air screaming, "They hurt my arms, they hurt my arms!"

That usually ended our efforts for the day. Meanwhile, Elliott was taking swimming lessons at the Venetian Pool, a large, beautiful public swimming facility in Coral Gables. Realistically, Sarah and I didn't expect him to learn to swim, but we were certain that the lessons would give him additional assurance and help to strengthen the leg muscles which he needed to walk. I continued to hope.

Meanwhile, this was the spring of 1942, the nation was at war, and the streets of Miami were filled with the bobbing caps of servicemen. Eddie came to visit us as Elliott was recovering from an uncomplicated bout with the mumps. Eddie enjoyed the respite from work, and it wasn't long before Elliott resumed his outdoor activities.

We all gathered in the yard after lunch and I said, AShow daddy how nicely you've learned to walk on your crutches, Elliott. Go ahead, show daddy."

Elliott peered at Eddie, Sarah, and me. For a minute he appeared quite serious. Then he replied, AOK, I'll walk for daddy."

Together we gazed intently while Elliott put his crutches in place. Then, to our utter disbelief, he proceeded to walk around the house with the aid of his crutches! He stumbled, his movements were not smooth, but he was walking—albeit on crutches. Yes, clumsily, unsteadily, not well-balanced, but joyfully, he was walking! After countless exercises, incessant prodding, daily encouragement, and the determination of a brave little boy, Elliott was indeed walking.

"I can't believe it," Eddie said.

"Look at him!" Sarah shouted.

"That's a good boy, Elliott," I shouted. "That's wonderful."

Eddie and I sat together outside, long after Elliott and Sarah had gone to bed. Today had been a milestone. Words were not necessary. Our youthful joys of marriage had matured after all we had been through together, and now, on the quiet evening of this eventful day, Eddie and I shared a real joy. We had courage for the future, wherever it would lead. Although we did not talk about our feelings often, we were always working together toward the goal of Elliott's happiness.

Then Eddie returned to Pennsylvania, and I was left to care for Elliott. One of the hardest things at that time was the coldness Elliott was experiencing from the other children. I bought ice cream, candy, cookies, and, in fact, everything children love to eat, all in the hopes that they would come play with Elliott. Unfortunately, none of it worked and Elliott remained a lonely little boy.

Then one day in September of 1942, I received a letter informing me that my mother had suffered a severe stroke and was dying. I had to leave for West Virginia immediately.

I called Sarah. "Would you please take care of Elliott while I'm gone? He knows you, and I don't have anyone else to leave him with," I said.

"Don't worry," she replied. "I'll take care of him."

As it turned out, I arrived in West Virginia in time for my mother's funeral. Afterwards, I decided to go to Pennsylvania to see Eddie for a short time.

When I returned to Miami, I went to pick up Elliott at Sarah's house.

"I'm sorry, Mrs. Weiss," Sarah told me. "Elliott isn't feeling very well."

Elliott was as jaundiced as he was when he was a baby. It turned that she had been feeding him a largely vegetarian diet, and it wasn't agreeing with him. Fortunately, it wasn't anything serious, and Elliott was soon back to normal once I took him home and returned him to his usual diet. Less than two weeks later, I had good news for Elliott: "Daddy is coming home to live with us."

Eddie had called with the news that he had sold the new pharmacy and was now moving to South Florida for good.

Chapter 9

In order for Elliott to be exposed to a normal educational environment and to other children, I did extensive research into private kindergartens. I was asked to remain in the classroom with Elliott for a while to see if he could adjust to the class before a permanent arrangement could be determined. These people did not have the faintest idea what cerebral palsy was, and they did not seem interested in learning about the disability. Elliott was not classified as a normal student. He constantly shifted in his seat, determined to get up and wander around. Not surprisingly, Elliott did not stay long at any of the schools. The teachers were not patient and their attitude reflected this feeling. As a result, the weekly tuition was being wasted. I became discouraged and decided to keep Elliott at home for a while. I purchased some books to work with him on his own level, and I let him play with Mary Ann, the little girl who lived next door.

Twice a week, I once again took Elliott, who was now about five years old, to the Venetian Pool for swimming lessons. Although he never mastered the techniques of the strokes, the exercise was good for strengthening his muscles.

Our friends, Bill and Lil Kotler, often came to take Elliott on outings, as well as to take us shopping. Bill, a self-employed carpenter, would let Elliott watch him make things. One item was a large wooden stroller for Elliott so that I could take for long walks through the neighborhood because Elliott couldn't cover any long distances on his crutches.

Mary Ann's mother was very understanding and kind-hearted. She encouraged her daughter to play with Elliott. What a wonderful feeling to be accepted!

Around this time, Eddie's sisters, Esther and Sadie, wrote that they were coming to visit and to look for a home. Each had a child who would be ready for college the next year. They both quickly found homes close to where we lived, and then it wasn't long before other members of the Weiss family followed.

Later that summer, Eddie's brother Emil paid us a visit. He also wanted to relocate in Miami. Eddie, Emil, and I found a beautiful two-bedroom duplex across the street from Coral Way Elementary School, where we planned to enroll Elliott. The east side of the duplex was vacant, so Emil's family moved in, but Eddie and I had to wait until the tenant's lease expired before we could move into our side of the duplex.

Shortly after our move, Emil and Essie divorced and left Miami. They rented their side to Peggy, the sister of the late Grace Kelly, Princess of Monaco, and her naval husband. We became great friends. Peggy had a lot of patience with Elliott and gave him a lot of attention. Her schooling in the parochial school had system taught her love and compassion for all mankind, including the disabled.

Whatever chore Peggy was engaged in, Elliott followed her. He would try to help her as much as he could, but she joked with him and took time out for a drink of Coke and cookies. Elliott would help her pull the weeds in the yard and would help her hang the laundry from the clothesline. Elliott and Peggy became such good pals, but then the Navy pulled all their forces out of Miami and they had to move back to Philadelphia. Then our days seemed so empty until it was time for Elliott to begin school again. I purchased a four-seater swing set and served refreshments in order to entice the neighborhood children use our yard as a playground, hoping that Elliott could make some friends. For a while, this seemed to be working out fine, but before the summer had ended, it was clear that the children were there for the free food and the new play equipment. When Elliott would go to their homes, he found that he was not welcome.

In September, the time came to register Elliott for first grade. Our beautiful new home, with its airy front screened porch and its many fruit trees, had taken on an air of excitement. We no longer had the financial worries of private schooling, and we now lived in a neighborhood with thirteen children about Elliott's age. Our luck had shifted, or so we thought. We truly believed the time was right for a new positive beginning at Coral Way Elementary, which was just cross the street from our new home.

If Elliott could find just one child who would become a real friend and companion, it would have meant so much to us. A whole new world would open up for him. But maybe that was too much for us to hope for.

Our next door neighbors, Bob and Edie Schweitzer, had a son named Howie, who was one year younger than Elliott. At first the two boys played rather well together. Bob, was still in the service, giving Eddie and myself a lot of time to spend together. We shared babysitting duties so we could each have a free evening one night per week. We also shared taking the boys with us on our grocery trips.

However, for reasons we never fully understood, when Bob returned home the friendship between our families ceased, so Elliott and I kept busy with our own family. Aunt Tillie and Uncle Julius visited us often. They took us shopping and to places where we could see new and interesting things such as the shore in Miami Beach, the Crandon Park Zoo, and many of the other beautiful recreational areas in South Florida.

When registration day finally arrived, Eddie and I walked Elliott to the school and waited in the registration line. Nervously, I crossed my fingers in hopes that all would go well. Elliott looked so handsome in his bright new shirt and pants, and in his beautiful new leather shoes, which I had shined to perfection. He had a big smile for his new teacher.

When it was finally our turn, we were greeted by the registrar who quickly told us they could not accept a child on crutches. He was considered handicapped and would have to attend a special schoolCthe Roosevelt School for Exceptional ChildrenCoperated under the Dade County Public School System with grades one through seven. Another great disappointment had crushed our dreams that Elliott could finally fit into a mainstream educational program.

After calling the Roosevelt School that same day, I quickly learned the procedure. Elliott would be picked up by bus at 8:00 a.m. and would not be returned home until 4:00 p.m. A cafeteria would provide lunches, but in order to have breakfast at home and get dressed on time, I had to get Elliott up by 7:00 each morning. At this point, Elliott was wearing long braces prescribed by the Crippled Children's Society. They were strapped at the hips and ankles and required 20 minutes to adjust them to his body.

So when school started the next day, I woke Elliott up, helped him get dressed, put on his braces, and helped him with his bathroom business. By the time I'd seen him onto the school bus and placed his crutches underneath the seat, I was emotionally exhausted and physically drained. Life was getting crueler for us by the day. Our dream of Elliott going to school across the street from our new home had turned into a frustrating nightmare. We had chosen the ideal home and location but the wrong school!

Roosevelt School was a pink art deco building built in 1925. It had beautiful tile floors and its ceilings gave it a feeling of grandeur that often reminded me of the Carlson School in Pompano Beach. It was formerly a private club and had been purchased by the school board to be converted into a school for disabled children.

Fortunately, Eddie's health was improving, so he started to look for work, and before long he received a phone call from the Alton Road Pharmacy, a large, modern store in Miami Beach. He was interviewed, offered a job, and he promptly accepted.

The end of World War II signalled the return home of many service-men and their families, bringing an influx of people to the Miami area. Thousands of servicemen from up north had trained in Miami Beach, and many decided to return when the war ended. In addition, many parents of discharged war veterans were among the new arrivals, causing the real estate market to flourish even more. Realtors would gather for lunch at the drug store where Eddie worked to discuss the numerous opportunities to buy and sell properties for a quick profit. We were lucky to get into some of those deals, and for a short while, Eddie and I owned part of a hotel, an apartment house, and some commercial property. All of these investments were modest money-makers.

Saturday nights for us were usually busy. Our house was filled with relatives—usually Uncle Harry and Aunt Peppy, along with their daughters and their families. Sometimes they would play a game of poker. Elliott was so excited about family because they would always bring treats or games for him.

All the neighborhood children had tricycles or bicycles. To help him keep up with the other children, we purchased a bright red tricycle for Elliott, which he learned to ride immediately.

The school routine was new and the days were long, but Elliott seemed fascinated with going to the big white school and being in first grade. His excitement, however, was short-lived, for he soon discovered he was at school to learn and not to play. Elliott just did not relish sitting in his seat for any length of time, and he quickly learned that by raising his hand he could be excused to go to the bathroom. This became a frequent occurrence and the teacher finally requested that Elliott be examined by a doctor to rule out any kidney or bladder problems. Tests proved the problem wasn't medical. Our son simply could not apply himself. Fearing failure made it easier for him to avoid trying.

For the next two years, Elliott was kept in the first grade. None of his teachers had the Amagic key" to unlock the door. "He seems to have it in him, but I don't know how to get it out of him," was how his teachers typically put it.

At the same time, Elliott was facing other problems; he was still finding it difficult to be accepted by the neighborhood children. His tricycle was good exercise for him and perhaps offered him a little more locomotion and independence than did his crutches. Elliott would speed around the block to visit the neighbors. I watched him struggle eagerly for friendship, yet he failed to find one real friend among the many children living in our area.

Why wasn't there just *one* child with the understanding to really like Elliott and have the patience to get to know him? Was it so difficult for another small child to realize how much Elliott needed another child's love and companionship? I learned very well how thoughtless and cruel normal children could be.

"You're crippled," a child would cry out to Elliott. Then Elliott would strike out at him with a crutch or simply run home in tears, hobbling furiously on both crutches.

Despite Elliott's speech and motor handicaps, Dr. Carlson had diagnosed his mentality as normal, and I was convinced that relationships with normal children would be important to his growth and maturity. We regularly invited children to our home, and many days they supposedly came over to play with Elliott in our large, screened-in porch. Elliott was eager for their companionship until they began to tease him.

One day I saw little Susie pick up a baseball and deliberately throw it at Elliott. It struck him in the center of his forehead. Quickly, I ran over and slapped Susie's hand, AWhatever do you mean hitting Elliott that way?" I scolded.

"Elliott's always kicking me, Mrs. Weiss," she said tearfully. "Sometimes I just can't stop from getting back at him." Immediately, I realized that I had been unfair to another child out of my pain for Elliott. I apologized to Susie and her mother.

Despite all the playground equipment in the backyard, the large assortment of toys, and the plentiful supply of cookies, candy, ice cream and drinks we purchased, they were not enough to buy the friendship of the other children. We finally decided friendship must come naturally or not at all. Sadly, those special childhood friendships never came.

Chapter 10

Roosevelt School offered many facets for the disabled children. Physical, speech, and occupational therapies were offered on a weekly basis through the Crippled Children's Society. In the classroom, each teacher had about 15 students, so personal attention was impossible. Elliott's homeroom teacher reported, "He is overly emotional." Much to our frustration, Elliott was developing the same psychological problems that Dr. Carlson had warned us about. But since Elliott's birth, there were no indications that he might suffer from mental deficiency. He smiled at 3 weeks old, laughed at 3 months old, and drank from a cup with some help at 8 months old, a progressions comparable to other children his age.

On a positive note, we had a friendly neighbor, Fred, whose last name I can't recall these many years later. Fred had a lot of patience with Elliott and taught him many of the tricks about carpentry and camping. Fred often took his grandchildren camping and fishing, and to our delight, he began to include Elliott on some of this trips. Fred was a sweet, retired gentleman who stayed at home a lot to work on his hobbies.

As soon as Elliott arrived home from school, he would head for Fred's house to see what he was making that day. Fred enjoyed the company and was glad to have an audience because his wife was often out or busy in the kitchen. Fred explained every carpentry tool and technique and he would often let Elliott try his skill at hammering nails. He showed him how to fold up a tent, and listed all the equipment they would need for each trip. The food supply was very important and he made a list of items that were needed from the market. He also taught Elliott about fishing. He explained the right kind of bait to use and what sort fish they were likely to catch.

One bright sunny day after Elliott got off the bus and had a drink of Coke, he went out to explore. This time it was a new adventure. About two hours had elapsed before I finally heard the familiar click of his crutches. Elliott had walked for the first time to Coral Way to visit Joe Toth, who ran a plant and nursery store. That was quite a hike for Elliott—the determining force to get there on his own was quite a milestone in his young life. He needed this confidence and he needed to communicate with someone he knew. He also needed to get there on his own legs. He made many trips after that first visit. Each time, Joe would call me and tell me Elliott had arrived and not to worry about him. I was pleased to know that they enjoyed each other's company.

Frances Huggins, the Roosevelt School principal, had a very active board of which I was a member. I was present at their annual Holiday Tea. The guest list included the mayor of Miami, principals of other schools, and other important members of the community. All holidays were heavily promoted to gain the public's attention, for Roosevelt was a special school, the only one of its kind in Miami. Mrs. Huggins was very devoted to the school and loved all her students.

Jane Collette, Elliott's first grade teacher, gave Elliott all satisfactory and even some excellent grades. In addition, he was making good progress in his physical activities. So how were we to know he wasn't learning anything? We were disillusioned by the fact that we had put forth so much effort to help our son, and good report cards made us believe that his years at the Roosevelt School were not fruitless. What was the major problem? Why didn't anyone have any answers?

After two years of frustration in the first grade, Elliott was refused a social promotion. I immediately wrote to Dr. Carlson, who agreed to re-enter him for another year in his program. That June, Eddie and I flew Elliott to Dr. Carlson's school in East Hampton.

After analyzing the money involved in buying our home, the promising report cards, and teachers telling us how well Elliott was doing academically, we decided to sell the house and move back to Pennsylvania. Maybe our luck would change. Maybe Florida held bad promises for us. During our time there, we had found no answers— only mixed feelings.

But the wrath of the winter winds and the snows of Pennsylvania, combined with the separation from our son, depressed Eddie and me. We prayed together each morning for a better life and a happy family, Eddie with his prayer book and I with my hands clasped. Eddie, with his happy memories of a large family and I with mine, longed for eventual stability in our family.

Once again, Elliott progressed at the Carlson School. A one-to-one basis always helped him to absorb and retain the knowledge that he was taught. Dr. Carlson could not understand why the teachers at Roosevelt could not reach him. "Either they are unqualified to teach special education or they just never took the time to understand the extent of Elliott's brain damage."

Along with the other students from the Carlson School, Elliott was transported to the Pompano Beach facility in the late fall. We were very anxious to see him again, to gaze at his boyish face and his beautiful smile, and to note how tall he had grown.

As Eddie continued to lose weight, his health problems increased, and my nervous system suffered from all the emotional upsets we had experienced. Eddie blamed his physical problems on the emotional upsets, so he found a good doctor who helped get his nervous system in better shape. We decided it was time for a discussion about what direction to take and formulate some concrete plans for our future.

We decided that the time was right for us to drive back to Miami and purchase a new home that would also give us some income. Eddie would look for work a few days per week. Luckily, we found a reliable real estate man, who found the ideal place for us on S.W. Sixth Street. The units in this pair of duplexes each had two bedrooms and a bath, a living and dining area, and a small back porch. It was ideal. We would live in one unit and rent out the others to help defray the expense of the school for the balance of the six months. Our hearts were full of great hopes with glowing reports of Elliott's progress in school. He was prepared for third grade and had high expectations for his future. Once again, we were on Acloud nine," but as usual, there were always more complications.

For starters, the two duplexes we purchased were filled with difficult tenants. Joe, who was a painter, gave us a worthless rent check, and then a few days later he moved out at midnight without notifying us. Isabelle, who lived in a front apartment, turned out to be a drug-addicted call girl. One evening one of her "customers" beat her up and we found her on the ground outside of her apartment bleeding and cry-ing. We sent her to the hospital to get treatment.

With Eddie working, I was responsible for handling the rentals. It wasn't easy work. Our tenants came from all walks of life, and we quickly learned that this was a difficult way to acquire money.

In January, Elliott again joined us to live at home. It turned out that Dr. Carlson had over-evaluated Elliott, which is to say that he thought Elliott would eventually be mainstreamed and could even go to college someday. At this point, Dr. Carlson admitted that Elliott was no longer making any progress. This over-evaluation was due in part to Elliott's physical conditioning, which had surpassed that of most of his peers. As a result, Elliott would return to Roosevelt since that was the only school in the area which he would be permitted to attend.

In the meantime, my brother Bill, his wife Edith, and their daughter Marilyn had moved down from Charleston, West Virginia. They stayed with us for a few weeks until they found a home in Coral Gables. Then Bill opened a men's store, University Men's Shop, which included a tuxedo rental service. Elliott became attached to his Uncle Bill in a short period of time and called him frequently on the phone. Bill would kid him about helping out in the store when he got older, but Elliott took him seriously.

One Saturday Elliott was walking around outside and talking to the neighbors. I called him in for lunch. After calling his name several times with no response, I became worried. Elliott was nowhere to be seen. He had never strayed from home before. My first thought was to call the police. I gave them a full description of Elliott and they promised to call me if he was found. To my relief, within half an hour I received a phone call. Elliott had been found at the bus station downtown and was being driven home.

His story was very interesting. He had wanted to go to Coral Gables to help his Uncle Bill in his store, but he didn't understand that bus fare was required in order to ride the bus. Even so, he did get onto a bus, but unfortunately, the bus he'd boarded was headed the wrong way. After a short talk, I helped Elliott to realize that what he'd done was wrong. Privately, however, Eddie and I were happy because Elliott's desire to do something productive showed us his determination; we were convinced that with time and effort, Elliott might accomplish many things.

Ronnie and Al, our tenants in the second apartment, were from Chicago. After a few months, their story about their severely retarded daughter unraveled. Their girl had been placed in an institution in their home town because the medical reports indicated she could never learn anything and probably never walk or talk. She was considered a vegetable. Usually they did not tell anyone about Joanna, but after meeting Elliott, Ronnie chose to confide in us. Ronnie soon became pregnant and they looked forward to having a normal child. On schedule, Ronnie gave birth to a beautiful baby boy who became the light of their life, and consequently they moved to larger quarters.

Subsequently, Hansie, her mother, and her photographer husband, Werner, who was from Haiti, moved into the vacant apartment. Since Hansie and Werner both worked, Hansie's mother spent most of her time cooking and cleaning. We became good friends and she gave me some of her prized recipes from Europe. For Elliott's birthday, Werner insisted on taking some pictures of Elliott and presented them to us as a gift. It was exciting to receive such a beautiful and professional gift. We all celebrated with birthday cake and ice cream.

While Eddie was working in Coral Gables, another real estate opportunity came our way. It was an eight-unit apartment building in Coral Gables that housed naval servicemen.

In the fall, Elliott re-entered Roosevelt School in the third grade. He had learned to read, write, and do simple arithmetic, but academically, he was not willing to apply himself beyond that. In spite of the private tutoring he had received at Carlson, he was not doing his classwork as quickly as the other children. His study habits were poor, and he had difficulty in accepting his responsibilities.

One report from a teacher, Eunice Kimbrough, stated, AElliott has a very sweet, happy disposition and is a capable boy. However, he needs to learn to depend on himself and to develop a willingness to work. His short span of attention, his dependence, and his refusal to accept any personal responsibility are keeping his academic and social development at a very unsatisfactory level."

The following report noted that, AHe is making more of an effort to succeed in his schoolwork. He is beginning to accept the responsibility for caring for his supplies and for getting to the bus on time. During short spasmatic periods, Elliott has shown that he can apply himself to schoolwork and make progress. However, these periods are too short and far apart to suggest any consistent gains. Elliott has shown some improvement. Ms. Kimbrough believes he is waking up and she hopes for a big improvement in the next semester."

The report cards from school, which arrived monthly, always indicated something along the lines of, "Elliott has it in him, but we don't know how to get it out of him." Strange how these words were repeated each month. Couldn't someone open Elliott's intricate brain and find out why it was not functioning in a normal fashion? We had so many questions but very few answers!

Chapter 11

With Elliott busy at Roosevelt School, my frustrations came out in a different fashion. During the balmy warm days of October, I called a few parents that I had heard about from various sources and invited them to my home to discuss the possibility of a parent association. Several parents attended, but one father in particular, Irving Goldman, who was very concerned about his son's future, became my co-founder of the Cerebral Palsy Parents Association. After several meetings our membership grew too large for my living room to accommodate.

Around the corner from my apartment there was a yellow building that housed a the Miami Spiritual and Metaphysical Church's large membership. They opened their doors to us and said we could use their facilities at no charge any evening when they did not have prayer meetings or healings. Happy and grateful for their generosity, we agreed to use the church's facilities on a monthly basis at no charge.

The general consensus of our group was that we were mainly interested in starting a physical therapy clinic. After calling a number of churches, (the location of the metaphysical church wasn't suitable for the clinic) I found a sympathetic ear, Minister Lillian, who generously offered use of an empty room in his church's basement. And so the White Temple Methodist Church's basement in downtown Miami become the base for our clinic. The beautiful art deco church with its pink buildings was huge and had many classrooms which we utilized weekly. A massage table, which was donated by the Polio Foundation, would bring us closer to our goal, but we did not yet have the funds to hire a therapist.

Minister Lillian asked the parents in our group to bring their children to the church for a healing. She also informed us that once a month she did psychic readings. Out of curiosity, I went to her on a Sunday to have her give me a reading. To my amazement, she blurted out AMinnie," which was my deceased mother's name, and then proceeded to tell me things about Elliott, although she never met him.

As we continued to meet monthly, Minister Lillian told us that we could probably attract a therapist to our group by having the newspaper come in and do a story about our organization. Since she was a psychic, Minister Lillian asserted that a story in the newspaper would open the door for us. Since the *Miami Herald* was our only hope, I called the editor and he sent out a reporter and photographer to my home to do the story, complete with pictures. The following Sunday, the *Miami Herald* ran a one-half page feature on our clinic.

"Miami's Forgotten Children Are Going to Get a Break." That was the caption of the story published on April 25, 1948. The article read as follows:

"Parents of children afflicted with cerebral palsy have organized in the hope of rehabilitating some of Miami's 500 youths crippled and distorted by this dreadful malady. Through its long-range program, The Cerebral Palsy Association, Inc. hopes to establish a training school where spastics can be given special attention both medically and intellectually. It wants a separate building to be operated, perhaps in conjunction with The Crippled Children's Society.

"On its immediate agenda is a physical therapy clinic to be held twice weekly, commencing in May, in a room provided by the White Temple Methodist Church. To date, the Cerebral Palsy Association, Inc. has a record of 150 Miami spastics, but based on the national average it is certain that 500 cerebral palsy victims in the greater Miami area under 20 years of age can benefit from the program. The clinic is expected to bring other spastic cases to the association's attention.

"At present, care of spastics is inadequate everywhere. This is not surprising because it is only recently that surveys, classifications, mental testing, and physical diagnosis of spastics have been on a sufficiently large scale to evaluate the problem. With proper attention, thousands of these unfortunate children can be rehabilitated and prepared to lead happier lives. From the Miami Cerebral Palsy Association's efforts, it is hoped that a national foundation might spring."

Along with this publicity was a picture of me and Elliott. There was also a story about Gene Boeninger, a law student, and about his fight to become self-sufficient. Today, Gene runs his own printing firm. Gene Boeninger, age 21 and the son of one of our members, often came to our meetings when we first organized. The story of Gene's fight to carry on as a normal human being was featured along with our publicity.

"I have cerebral palsy," Gene wrote. "More specifically, I am a spastic. I have been this way all my life. My mother first noticed that something was wrong when I couldn't sit up normally at six months of age. Doctors told her that eventually I would overcome most of the difficulties which spastics have to endure. But most important of all, they recognized the fact that I had a normal mentality. That, in itself, was a milestone because it wasn't so many years ago that spastics were looked upon as being idiots and feeble-minded persons.

"As long as I can remember, I have been under some sort of treatment. Initially, my progress was slow. I could not dress myself, and when I wanted to go to the lavatory somebody always had to help me. In school I was like most other children. Although I was a smart child, it couldn't be seen in most of my work.

"From the start, spelling and reading were my favorite subjects and also my best, but as I grew older, the importance of all aspects of my education became clearer. I gradually came to like school sufficiently to improve my grades and really get down to work. In both grammar and high school there was a separate room for the handicapped where one of two physical therapists were in attendance. We were given exercises to do and some speech correction. I have always been able to feed myself, so my parents haven't had to worry in that direction. But it took eleven years before I could completely dress myself, including buttoning my shirts and tying my shoes. I still have difficulty in closing my shirt collars, however.

"Today I drive my own car and run a printing business in Miami. I will obtain my Bachelor of Business Administration degree in 1949 and law degree from the University of Miami two years later. The very fact that I am a university student makes me realize all the more how lucky I am to be living in this day and age. It wasn't too long ago that victims of cerebral palsy, as I mentioned previously, were automatically assumed to be mentally deficient."

"The grotesque features and drunken gait characteristic of so many spastics helped foster the impression to no end. The biggest difficulty was the fact that spastics could not talk, or if they could, it was often not intelligible except to the immediate family and constant companions.

"Today, doctors are very much aware that spastics possess an average, and in many instances, superior intelligence. In order to bring it to the surface, education should be started at a normal age, and it should not be a standard type, but should fit the child's interests and special needs. If the child becomes disinterested, it is sometimes difficult to for that child to catch up. Therefore, constant monitoring, planning, and adjustments to the educational plan are critical.

"The unfortunate truth is that cerebral palsy is not a rare condition. In fact, it occurs quite regularly in the population at the rate of seven per 100,000 a year in each age group, out of which one dies before the age of development of the brain during pregnancy. In some cases, vitamin deficiencies, glandular disturbances, syphilis, and other systemic diseases during pregnancy are responsible, but most often the cause is the result of some complication during and after birth. Premature and rapid delivery, the use of forceps with heavy pressure, and complications due to the RH factor in the parents' blood, and many other complications are major factors. After birth, convulsions, encephalitis (a type of sleeping sickness), and accidents involving the head may also cause cerebral palsy.

"*Spastic paralysis* is the name of one of the major subdivisions of cerebral palsy. Other types of neuro-muscular crippling conditions included in the general category of cerebral palsy are *athetosis*, or the presence or involuntary motion; *ataxia*, or balance and primary disturbances of coordination; and *rigidity*, or a stiff, lead-like condition of the muscles. These conditions vary considerably, and there is no single type of treatment for cerebral palsy as a whole.

"In treating the various conditions, surgery is not the only answer. Physical therapy, occupational therapy, braces, and drugs are also vital. The most important thing to remember is that the earlier the treatment is begun, the less time bad habits will have to form.

"Four out of six cases are definitely treatable, but two out of the six cases involve feeble-mindedness and require permanent custodial care. The four treatable cases can be divided into three subdivisions. One case will be severely handicapped, homebound, and essentially hopeless from the point of view of physical rehabilitation. Another case will be so mild that any prolonged degree of treatment is unnecessary. Two cases will be moderately handicapped and capable of great improvement. The two cases requiring permanent custodial car are obviously the most severe forms."

As a result of Gene Boeninger's newspaper article, a European physical therapist offered her volunteer services and an orthopedist from Coral Gables agreed to examine the children and prescribe the treatments free of charge. All the furniture and supplies we needed were sent to the church. We were in business!

But then many sad events transpired among our group. One father took his five-year-old daughter's life along with his own by immersing themselves in deep canal. Jerry, a young man of 25, who rode his three-wheel bike to my home daily to talk with me in his slurred speech was unable to walk, but I arranged for our doctor to examine him. On his next visit, he informed me that the doctor said he was too old to benefit from treatment. Tragically, his body was found in the Miami River the following day. His bike was also found on the banks of the river some distance away.

Immediately I was tormented by these tragedies and the fear that the same thing would eventually happen with Elliott. I could see my son's increasing frustration and inability to learn, despite the tests that showed he has a normal mentality.

Most of our members' children were severely impaired. In fact, only a few could walk. The children sometimes came with their parents to meetings in their mother's arms. Several of our patients suffered from epilepsy and most of them had never attended school because of their handicaps. They never had been exposed to any kind of treatment. By comparison, Elliott was fortunate and blessed.

Charlotte, one of our charter members, told us about her daughter's tragic birth. Forceps were used and she suffered severe brain damage that left her unable to walk or talk. Although she had been checked by Dr. Winthrop Phelps in Baltimore, there was not much hope for her condition and this affected her parents quite severely. Charlotte's husband died early from a heart attack, but Charlotte continued to work with us for quite some time.

"fter several months of our organization's demonstration for the need, we were convinced the National Council of Jewish Women to adopt our clinic as a community project. We rented a large storeroom in the southwest section of Miami, and they provided us with a full-time registered therapist and volunteers to answer the phone and manage the office.

They booked all the appointments on a small-scale payment basis, and we raised some monies to cover expenses. First, our patients were examined by the orthopedists who then referred them to the clinic with instructions for treatment. The clinic remained in operation until the United Cerebral Palsy's national organization formed and took over the operation of the existing clinic. It was not long before they built a new, modern facility adjacent to Cedars of Lebanon Hospital near downtown Miami. We were proud to have laid the groundwork for them.

Chapter 12

Although Elliott attended classes at each day at Roosevelt, he was still struggling to acquire an education. He was promoted to the fourth grade socially. His fourth grade teacher, Margaret Jones, reported he was doing better, but that Elliott wasted too much time. "I constantly have to remind Elliott to sit in his seat, his spelling is very poor, and he frequently forgets to do his homework. It's very frustrating, but I just can't seem to get through to him."

Not surprisingly, at the end of fourth grade, Elliott was once again given a social promotion.

Through the efforts of The Crippled Children's Society, a prominent specialist in the field of cerebral palsy was invited down to Miami to examine the children with this affliction, since at the time there was no qualified doctor anywhere in the state of Florida, with the possible exception of Dr. Carlson, who only examined students coming into his boarding school.

Dr. Winthrop Phelps of Baltimore had his own boarding school and clinic. He was often called upon to examine and give his diagnosis throughout the United States. He diagnosed Elliott as a rotary athetoid. This was quite different from Dr. Carlson's report. Dr. Phelp's report read: "He walks with a wide base gait and some unsteadiness. Heel cords adequate length. Hip joints are in normal position in sockets. No limitations of rotation of hip flexion or extension. Abduction fairly strong. External rotators are normal. Internal rotators are apparently weak. Strengthening work should be done in a very internal rotation."

We had just celebrated Elliott's 11th birthday. He was a handsome child, and many friends and relatives joined us in our fun. He had been taking more interest in his school work and one teacher reported that she believed he was "waking up." So much effort had been spent trying to find the key to motivate him, so this was very welcome news. New hope rose within me. And then one day Elliott came home from school and said: "Here, mother, take my crutches and put them away. I won't need them anymore."

"Our son is walking, our son is walking alone," I shouted to Eddie when he arrived home from work. "Look, Eddie, I put his crutches in the garage." Even though he was tired from a hard day at the drugstore, Eddie danced around the living room with me. We both kissed Elliott and gave him lots of hugs for his decision and for his courage and ability to walk alone.

When school opened in the fall, the handicapped children were placed under the medical and orthopedic care of The Crippled Children's Society. This time Dr. Harriett Gillette, a cerebral palsy specialist from Atlanta, was the attending physician. I was invited to observe the examination. Her diagnosis was a mixture of rotary athetoid and ataxia spastic. Physical therapy was recommended and high-laced shoes were prescribed. In occupational therapy, Elliott had to strive for dexterity. Speech therapy was also prescribed.

Some friends of ours had two children, one normal and one with cerebral palsy. We were invited to their home for birthday cake to celebrate when their normal child became one year old. Their older daughter was sitting in a wheelchair, unable to speak, but mentally alert. We noted the happiness on the faces of this mother and father and felt the great love radiating from all the members of the family for the healthy little toddler. I could think of nothing except the warmth I felt in their home. On the way home, Eddie and I decided it was time to add to our family. It was the birthday party that made up my mind.

The years of 1949 and 1950 brought us two major blessings. Elliott was walking on his own and we learned that we had a baby due in

October 1950. The house was bursting with excitement. There was so much to do and think about.

Because of my strong desire to help disabled children, I volunteered my services with The Crippled Children's Society. They welcomed me with open arms, for they knew my background with cerebral palsy. I was immediately made an honorary board member and put in charge of the AEaster Lily Day" collection. My first assignment was to take Elliott to see Sophie Tucker, a popular nightclub singer who was booked at a local club. I was to interview Ms. Tucker and accept her donation in the canister. The *Miami Herald* took the picture which appeared in the paper the following day.

Then came an opportunity for Eddie to open a small pharmacy in a medical building and he quickly jumped at the chance. The emotional challenge of having another business of his own was just the thing he needed to stimulate his interest in life again. My friendship with the president of the National Council of Jewish Women opened the door for us. Her husband was a medical doctor who had just built a clinic near the *Miami Herald*, and he was looking for a pharmacist to open the store in the space reserved for that purpose. Eddie opened his latest business with enthusiasm and it had the promise of becoming a profitable business. He only had to keep the doctor's hours, which were a reasonable five and a half days per week.

After Dr. Gillette examined Elliott again, she reported that his emotional problems were now becoming more pronounced as he was aging. He was experiencing severe temper tantrums. She recommended a new school in Alabama and we considered it for the future. We were both tormented by the report and started to think that Elliott might have some level of retardation. We had to look toward and perhaps find some permanent home for Elliott.

My search for a diagnosis and treatment of Elliott's condition was over at last. Now we knew what we were facing. Elliott had been treated by the best doctors. My refusal to accept the hopelessness which doctors had tried to force upon me had now, to a great degree, been rewarded. Elliott could talk, he could walk, and he was in a school program. Not all his physical or educational problems were solved, but most of them were out of my hands.

The following report by Dr. Seymour Blumenthal, a psychologist, was sent to us after his evaluation:

"On the Revised Stanford-Binet, Form L, Elliott attains a mental age of 8-4, and an IQ of 81, indicating dull-normal intelligence. His range of testing is from year Level VII through year Level X. His vocabulary development, as indicated by his ability to define words, is at the ten-year level of expectancy. His judgment and reasoning abilities are variable and, on the whole, quite immature. However, there are indications that there is a basically better range of ability in these areas. Retention is likewise variable with the concomitant of poor mental control as well as evidence of difficulty in learning for this reason.

"A series of performance tests were administered to this boy, but as was already known, Elliott's severe handicap is the use of his hands and fingers which do not permit for any comparison with known standards. On the basis of a qualitative evaluation of his functioning—partially out of the interference due to muscular difficulties—the boy indicates that his range of ability is of approximate range.

"In general, his development in the basic school skills of reading and arithmetic are not too well established. He has some simple word recognition, but it is not adequate for satisfactory comprehension in text materials; his ability along arithmetical lines is severely retarded.

"It is this examiner's impression that the present test results are not at all representative of his basic mental abilities. To a large extent, the present test results are a reflection of very poor habits which have been instituted in his study and general overall adjustment so that he does not at all make use of what appears to be at least average mental ability status. In general, he will not extend himself to give adequate impression of his basic mental ability structure. To a large extent, much of the present difficulty in adjustment, as well as in ineffective use of his basic mental abilities, must be attributed to over-protection and a lack of stimulation and motivation which would tend to make him more effective. The parents, while well-meaning, have done very little to install a plan of discipline which would make him a more effective child in line with his basic mental abilities. At the present time, the boy is infantile, demanding, and utilizes every avenue to control his parents and therefore avoids accepting responsibility which he can apparently handle. This dependence, and the advantage that he takes of his parents, will subsequently set a behavior pattern which will be most difficult to control and which, in general, will tend for maladjustment. Effective management as well as a specific plan of discipline for the child is of paramount importance.

"Recommendations: This is not a problem of intellective retardation, but rather interference in the use of his approximate average mental abilities due to personality problems which have been more or less conditioned by over-protection of the parents. He is, therefore, not effectively using his basic abilities and is presenting a very inadequate picture of them. His parents were counseled to formulate a plan which would be in line with the boy's abilities and wherein they would be able to maintain gradually increasing programs which make optimal use of his basic abilities for adjustment. From the school point of view, the boy is retarded in the basic school skills, but this likewise is a reflection of this boy's unwillingness to extend himself, which stems initially from home. If both the parents and school can coordinate their activities for an adequate plan of discipline for this child, a more effective adjustment should be noted. Remedial education should be instituted at the earliest opportunity."

Eddie and I never discussed our feelings about Elliott. It was like we were in a silent conspiracy not to speak out loud about how Elliott's problems affected us, as if the result of voicing our emotions would somehow make things worse. Eddie had suffered silently, often leaving the major action to me. I now look back and wonder if some of his silence had to do with a psychological rejection of the situation. Did he refuse to accept the facts of Elliott's world of reality? He was a kind and loyal husband, but he found it difficult to bare his soul.

Dr. Blumenthal's report gave us further insight into Elliott's condition and his possible future education. Apparently, Dr. Carlson had overestimated Elliott's capabilities, perhaps because our son was much younger then and more difficult to analyze.

Chapter 13

The days passed quickly during my nine months of pregnancy. I looked forward to the delivery of a normal baby, as well as getting back to my original size eight dress.

I was under special care of Dr. Leon Greene, our medical gynecologist friend who rented space in the physician's building where Eddie ran his pharmacy. He assured me that everything was normal and not to be concerned; he would take care of me just like he would his own daughter. During her last examination, Dr. Gillette had recommended a new summer camp for Elliott in the hills of North Carolina. She thought Elliott would benefit greatly from the camp. I kept busy by labeling his camp clothes and by preparing the layette for our expected newborn.

Elliott left for camp in June for two months. He flew alone but was monitored by the flight attendant and met by Travelers Aid to make sure he boarded the right bus for camp. The local newspaper took pictures and he was photographed getting off the plane in Blowing Rock. He was a celebrity!

Elliott had a wonderful experience at Camp Sky Ranch, which had just opened that summer for handicapped children. He had many stories to tell and took a lot of pictures with the Brownie camera which we bought for him because it was relatively easy to use. Nonetheless, many of his pictures were actually taken by others, once he had composed the shot.

September was a bustling time. We had to purchase a crib, a dressing table, and chest of drawers. It was going to be a tight fit for the small bedroom we had available, but we would manage until we had the money to buy a larger home. All the arrangements were made with

Sarah to stay with Elliott while I was in the hospital. She would also prepare the breakfast and dinner meals during that time.

Elliott was so excited about having a sister or brother in the family.
He had been the only child for almost twelve years. I had often thought
about having another child, but did not think I could cope with both
and do them equal justice. Elliott needed special time for his educational and emotional needs.

Elliott's twelfth birthday was in September. Family members came
over to celebrate with cake and ice cream and they brought some new
clothes for Elliott, too. By now they knew that the shirts Elliott wore
must be pull-ons and that his pants had to have an elastic waist.

The time for my delivery was getting closer, my stomach protruding
as if it housed an over-inflated basketball. I sensed that this child would
be a girl, although she was a powerful kicker. She just wanted to get out
into the new world. There was a lot more activity than with Elliott when
I had carried him. He had kicked very little and was rather light. For the
first time, I came to realize that whatever was wrong with Elliott had
begun while I was carrying him, and that the problems were only wors-
ened by the difficult nature of his delivery with Dr. Wilson.

I awoke that night to pitch darkness and was immediately alert. What
was it that had aroused me so quickly? Then I felt the cramp-like pain
low in my back. The time had come! I wanted to wake Eddie but
decided to wait a little while. It might be a long time and Eddie would
need all the rest he could get.

My mind was spinning. The pregnancy had been normal; I had not
experienced any nausea beyond what was normal for any woman during
the first three months. But as I lay in bed thinking of what this day might
bring, I knew I was terribly afraid of the final outcome. Could there be
something wrong with me that made it impossible for me to give birth
to a normal child? Would the birth process be handed skillfully? With
these thoughts clouding my mind, I was filled with increasing fear at the

approach of my child's birth. I was terrified that I would have to relive the unspeakable tragedy of Elliott's entrance into the world.

My body stiffened. I wanted to shout, "Damn that doctor in Pennsylvania!" It suddenly became clear that my anger toward Dr. Wilson had become deep and strong. I had kept my anger deep inside all those years, voicing only a cool but objective analysis of Elliott's birth. I had tried many times to find out what had gone wrong, but without success. I felt chills run up my spine as the pain came again. "God," I prayed. "Take away my rage! Help me to be reasonable. I know I am desperately afraid. Oh please, God, don't let it happen again, not again!"

I woke Eddie, dressed, and called Sarah to come and stay with Elliott. Then we were on our way to the hospital.

After the interminable storm passed, a nurse with a beaming smile placed into my arms the most beautiful baby girl I had ever seen. This tiny 6 1/2 pound child, whom we named Marlene, had arrived at 11:00 A.M. I could not believe that this porcelain doll with brushed up curls around the back of her head and a snookie roll of hair on the top was my baby. I thought they had made a mistake in the nursery, but the tiny row of plastic beads the size of a quarter said "Weiss." There was no error. She was our baby girl.

I fell into a light sleep. Later I was awakened by a kiss on my forehead. Eddie stood by my side with a big grin on his face, holding a dozen dark red roses in one hand and a package under his arm. "We're very lucky," he said smiling. Even if he had tried, there was no way he could have hidden the excitement, joy, and relief on his face and in his eyes.

"Eddie, this is the first time you have ever given me roses except for my birthday. And that package, you old dear, what have you brought me?"

He stood silently as I carefully untied the precious ribbon on the package. In the box was an exquisite blue nightgown. Our hands touched and, still in silence, our eyes met for a long moment.

A little later Eddie said, AFor 12 years, Rose, you have dedicated your life to Elliott. I'm sure your hope and courage have played a large role in seeing Elliott walk. And you have received the reward of his words, his speech. But what will happen now? Have you thought about what this new baby will do to our lives, especially Elliott's?"

"Well, you know I haven't been a pampering mother, have I?"

"No."

"Elliott will be more on his own now, as he will have to be anyway one day, and that is as it should be. You remember what a blow it was when we had to accept the fact that others could help him with some things better than you and I. To a great measure, from now on, what Elliott does will be up to Elliott."

"Don't worry about where Marlene will fit into this picture. I've already been dreaming what it will be like to raise a normal child. I'll dedicate my efforts to giving her a normal, happy life just as ardently as I have worked for Elliott. I'll make room in my life for both of them. Marlene must learn very early to respect and accept her handicapped brother."

Dr. Greene came into my room. "Congratulations on your beautiful, healthy, normal daughter." Dr. Greene went on to explain that he had done just a little cutting (an episiotomy) just to make sure everything would be fine. "She's also been examined by the pediatrician and he's given us a glowing report. Dr. Greene sat with me for a while and explained to me why I should not have had any previous problem delivering a normal baby. Then, I thought, it must have been something Dr. Wilson had done wrong which had caused Elliott's brain damage. But then again, I've had to accept that I'll never truly know what went wrong with my boy.

Each time I walked to the nursery to admire my baby, I noticed she was not in her crib but in the lap of the nurse while she was doing her charts. Stretched out on her stomach with the nurse patting her on the back, Marlene went to sleep. I knocked on the window to get the nurse's attention. I wanted to know why my baby wasn't in her bed. The nurse smiled at me and said, "Because she is the cutest one here, the pride of the nursery and a very good baby. She hardly ever cries."

To that, I replied, "OK, but don't spoil her too much."

At the end of the week, it was time to leave the hospital and go home. Uncle Julius and Aunt Tillie arrived shortly before lunch to escort us home. Aunt Tillie held Marlene tightly, for this baby was going to be her new love. Our small home was bursting at the seams. Sarah had decorated the living room with a big "Welcome" sign and had tied colorful balloons all over the room. It was a Saturday and Elliott was home too. A beautiful lunch was on the table and I felt like a queen for a day. Sarah, who now had a nurse's degree, had taken three weeks off from her job to care for Marlene. It was a wonderful gesture, for she was always in demand, but our friendship over the past twelve years had been steadfast. Since I brought her to Florida, despite the many changes in our lives, she had always remained grateful.

Marlene had the usual three-month colic. Eddie and I took turns at night walking her or pushing her carriage back and forth until she went back to sleep. Watching the growth of a normal child was a new experience for us. She did everything according to the book. She sat up at six months old and danced her version of the "hula" to Arthur Godfrey's guitar music, Hawaiian style. She played with her rattles and toys without any lessons or teachers. Everything came automatically. I told everyone there wasn't anything more interesting in this world than watching the development of a normal child. She was such a contrast to Elliott, and I didn't want to miss a moment of this pleasure. Marlene had her periodical examinations and immunizations at due times. At the age of one, she walked, could say "mama" and "dada," and even "bubba" for her brother. She loved to play with all her toys and even had a little girl to play with in the neighborhood.

That spring, Elliott completed his grades on a social level at Roosevelt and was transferred to the Ada Merritt Junior High School, where he was placed on a social level rather than on an academic level. Ada Merritt provided bus service and had special classrooms for the handicapped youngsters, as well as classes for mainstream students. It was at that point in his life when Elliott showed a renewed interest in carpentry. Ada Merritt did not use the report card system, but instead issued progress reports on a social scale. The classes were small and students graduated at 18 years of age. In fact, Elliott remained there until he turned 18, at which point he was awarded a social diploma. Today this is known as "aging out of the system."

Not knowing quite what to do with Elliott at that point, Eddie and I weighed the situation very carefully and decided to follow Dr. Gillette's advice to try the Charlanne School in Birmingham, Alabama. It was a new boarding school for the handicapped. Since it was a private school, this would mean smaller classes and more time per student. We were willing to take this last educational chance to see if Elliott would benefit. Perhaps some vocation would interest Elliott so that he could have a productive future. Therapy would also be included, so we hoped they would continue helping him with his walking, speech, and muscle coordination. So in September of 1956, Elliott flew to Birmingham to register for Charlanne's fall and spring semesters.

We kept in close touch with Elliott and received regular reports. They informed us that his academic work was improving. He was doing a little better in reading, and geography and science were of great interest to him. He was doing fourth-grade work in these two subjects and eagerly hunted for science stories in his *Weekly Reader*. His language comprehension was also on the fourth-grade level, and he seemed to understand sentence construction, correct usage of words, letter writing, and story telling.

Elliott's teachers at Charlanne believed he could make more rapid progress, but only if he would exert himself. They all agreed that he still needed encouragement if he was to achieve a higher level of independence, and that he needed coaching in initiative in high academic work and everyday activities.

Prior to Christmas vacation, Elliott was given the Stanford-Binet Intelligence Test and the results indicated he was normal mentally. It seemed the major cause of his problems was that he was a typical teenager who wasn't eager to apply himself. How I wanted to believe them! If the key to his learning difficulties could be found, then Elliott might have a profession he could pursue, despite his physical handicaps. Part of me continued to hope, but serious doubts continued to linger in my mind.

The progress report at the end of May seemed to be a bit more encouraging. "Elliott is reading in the new *If I Were Going* reader, which is a hard third- level reader. He interprets the contents of the stories with a great deal of exactness when the stories are read orally, but he is unable to give a very clear interpretation when the story has been read silently. Elliott enjoys Word Drill period, as he does nicely with the sounds of letters and the pronouncing of new words, and most of the time he interprets the correct meaning of the new words.

"Elliott seems to understand sentence construction, correct usage of words, letter writing, and story telling. Elliott has begun spelling on the fifth grade level, but this progress requires more time than he wishes to give; therefore, he is not too happy about his advancement in spelling. He has a very good conception of the use of the dictionary, arranging words in alphabetical order, and doing diction work. Elliott works at a very slow rate of speed when working independently."

"Elliott moved along faster in fourth grade arithmetic when he was adding and subtracting, but when he reached multiplication and division he made very slow progress. Elliott moves very slowly when working independently in arithmetic."

"The typewriter has been a joy to Elliott and a great help, too. He has shown a steady improvement in his use of the typewriter. He tried very hard to use the correct finger on the correct key and to learn the entire use of the typewriter. His typewriter has been a great help to him in his classroom studies. He has used it very successfully for work in geography, spelling, and language."

"We believe that Elliott could make more rapid progress with greater effort because he seems capable of better work than he does; however, Elliott does better and faster work when under complete supervision. However, independently he seems to progress at a slow rate of speed and lacks concentration. Without close supervision, he goes on to other activities instead of concentrating on the assigned work."

"He seems to enjoy collecting articles and is very appreciative of what is given to him, but he lacks determined effort to do things for himself at times. He seems to enjoy annoying other people and children younger than himself, but he will apologize when corrected. Efforts should be continued to help Elliott grow to become more independent in his work habits. We believe he has improved considerably this school year and has Agrown up" to a great extent, but, of course, he still needs encouragement to develop more independence and more initiative in his work and in his everyday activities."

Chapter 14

Dry-wood termites had invaded our current duplex, and so we had the place tented, but it only helped temporarily because the persistent little bugs returned again in the spring. Once again, it was time to look for a new, larger, home where we would be more comfortable.

Soon we found a newly-constructed home on Southwest 18th Avenue, which had been sitting vacant six months after its completion. "It's a big, beautiful home," Eddie said after he'd first seen the house, located in a neighborhood where he'd delivered some prescriptions. "Here's the number for the builder. Call them and arrange for us to see the inside." I followed Eddie's suggestion, and immediately I fell in love with the place. Within minutes I could visualize how the rooms would look furnished. The builder, Mr. Stevens, was anxious to sell the house, so he agreed to take our duplexes in trade, with the balance in cash. We were ecstatic. Now we had a new, large, permanent home, a new pharmacy, and a beautiful, normal daughter. We were also looking for peaceful solutions for Elliott's future. Indeed, we were beginning to feel very lucky.

I shopped for furniture for the three bedrooms, and after explaining the various pieces to Eddie he reluctantly nodded his head in approval. Within a few days I had found a French provincial bedroom set for Marlene and a white Italian provincial suite for our bedroom. For Elliott's room I purchased a single bed, bookcases, a desk for his type-writer, and a chest of drawers, all suitable for a typical teenage boy's room. We also bought a new table and chairs for the kitchen and a rattan set for the screen-enclosed front porch. To save some money, we decided that new furnishings for the living and dining rooms could wait until later, although we did buy a large new television set. Fortunately the garage already contained a brand new matching washer and dryer.

Shortly after we moved in, with Elliott's and Marlene's help, Eddie and I planted our victory garden in the large backyard. Our garden mainly consisted of beefsteak tomatoes, but we also planted carrots and assorted other vegetables.

We took time selecting the art work for our new home. We would shop on Saturdays after Eddie came home from the store. In addition to its annual art show, Coconut Grove, an area located at the southern end of Miami overlooking Biscayne Bay, was home to many beautiful galleries that we enjoyed shopping in.

Then Elliott, who was now twenty years old, came home again after his two-year tenure at Charlanne. We purchased an adult three-wheel bicycle for him so he could ride around and meet the neighbors. Unfortunately, despite our son's friendly efforts to meet new people, our neighbors just weren't receptive to Elliott. We just wished that Elliott could have found at least one young man in his age group to talk to or go places with. Just one friend would have made such a difference in his life. In this beautiful community that we loved so much, the same dark cloud began to appear on the horizon each beautiful day. While my heart filled with joy for Marlene, it ached for Elliott. Despite his disappointing efforts to make new friends, Elliott always remained upbeat and friendly and optimistic that he would eventually make new friends.

One day our neighbors informed me that a new family had purchased the white three-bedroom house across the street. The family consisted of three daughters, a teenager, a two-year-old, and a three-month-old baby. Marlene and I were elated—a playmate. Until now, we did not have any young children who lived in our immediate area.

A few days after our new neighbors moved in, I had my first encounter with Maxine, their two-year-old daughter. I wheeled Marlene over to their house after one of our afternoon strolls. As we entered the front porch, Maxine was staring at us through the screen door. As soon as I said "Hello," I heard the quick response, "Can I come over to your house to play?" I quickly answered, "Yes, we would love to have you."

Marlene and Maxine's new-found friendship was cemented quickly and they became fast friends. Jean, Maxine's mother, was also very friendly. We quickly learned that we shared a common bond; Jean's sister had been born with cerebral palsy. Jean worked side by side with her husband, Morris, at a supermarket in Miami, so our time together was limited. However, we did spend Wednesdays together with our girls. We would go to the beach, go toy shopping, or attend social activities that our girls were involved in.

Meanwhile, Elliott's daily bicycle rides continued to be more important to him because they gave him a sense of freedom, but the neighbors continued to shut their doors on him. As a result, Elliott began riding his three-wheeler down to Coral Way, where he met and visited some of the local merchants he'd met before his two years at Charlanne; some of the merchants were receptive to him, but others, of course, were not.

During this time, Eddie and I had a little more money at our disposal than we had previously. We enjoyed spending our Saturday afternoons with Marlene and Elliott, at various department stores around town, shopping for their clothing and other necessities. I still had not learned to drive, (that would come some years later) so in order to get around, I had to depend on Eddie, which was difficult, because he was spending so much of his time working. Something we enjoyed immensely were our frequent dinners at the Biscayne Cafeteria on Miracle Mile in Coral Gables, where we dined as often as two or three times a week.

In addition to our immediate family, more of Eddie's relatives from up north were migrating to Florida and settling in. We enjoyed the togetherness that this allowed us and we all got together whenever possible.

During this time, I was a member of the National Council of Jewish Women. I was faithful to the group because of the good fortune that came to us as the result of my acquaintance with one of the members, Sylvia Levin. Sylvia's husband was a well-established ophthalmologist in the Physician's Building on North Bayshore Drive. It was Dr. Levin who put Eddie in touch with the landlords of the building after suggesting that this would be a smart place for Eddie to open his new business. Although Eddie wouldn't get much walk-in traffic in such a store, it was clear that he would always be busy, filling prescriptions for patients seeing doctors in the building. Fortunately, Eddie took Dr. Levin's advice, and for about ten years he ran this successful pharmacy until he became too ill to continue working, at which point he sold off the inventory and shut the doors.

As a board member of the National Council of Jewish Women, I suggested that we collect educational toys for the pre-school kindergarten children in Israel at Hanukkah time. This project was named AShip a Box," and after much consideration, my suggestion was accepted and implemented on a national level.

While Elliott attended a two-week summer camp, Eddie, Marlene, and I went to a summer resort nearby in Asheville, North Carolina. Eddie decided to go to Duke University Medical Center to see if they could diagnose the burning sensation he had been experiencing in his tongue. As it turned out, the ensuing report was that Eddie had become diabetic. This news came as a shock to us at first, but then we finally accepted it as something else we would have to live with. Eddie's mother also had developed diabetes, so this was apparently a genetic misfortune and should not have come as much of a surprise.

Another health problem also presented itself at about the same time. Marlene presented the first evidence of asthma. Her first attack was brought on by her sleeping on a feather pillow. For a frightened moment, it seemed she might be less than healthy. Fortunately, however, her asthma has never been much of a hindrance. Marlene was an active child, and as an adult she continues to be an energetic and vibrant woman.

As she was growing up, I constantly marvelled at the easiness of Marlene's growth and maturity. As a student in school, she always understood everything that was being taught. She smiled whenever anyone spoke to her and I always marvelled at her precise coordination. As a child, our daughter was full of love and laughter and every day she brightened our household with her countenance.

One day I entered the living room and found Eddie lying on the sofa with the evening paper discarded on the stool beside him. He seemed not to notice me, but then he said quietly, "Sit down, Rose. It's time we took a good look at where we are with Elliott. He has been in so many schools—very good schools—Charlanne being one of them."

"Eddie," I said to him. "What are you getting at?"

"I'm just pointing out the reality: Elliott is 21 years old now and he's still functioning on a third grade level. What does that tell us, Rose? Let's be truly honest with each other about this for once. Of course we both want so much to believe that the magic key will be found to change things, but how far are we supposed to take this fantasy that he's going to suddenly get well? Where else is there to turn? All these years I've watched you devote your energy to searching, working, and studying how to help Elliott. You've had so little of your own life. As long as your efforts and the special schools were helping him, I had no problem, but I've begun to wonder how much of this has been worth it. I just can't stand to see Elliott pushed anymore. I don't say a lot, Rose and you know I've gone along with you, even though it meant keeping us drained financially. But let's face it. Deep down you know as well as I that although no authority has had the courage to tell us, we must accept—we must face the truth that—"

Eddie was struggling to say it but kept avoiding the word. I finally interrupted him by finishing his statement. "Elliott is retarded."

"Yes, that's right, Rose. I'm sorry, but Elliott is retarded."

Both of us were quiet for a long moment, letting the fact take shape.

"Eddie, it truly seems to me now that all the testing, the reports, and the remarks uttered by the string of professionals we've consulted are a shapeless mass of meaningless words. No one—not one—has provided us with a solution. For a long time I've been studying the school reports and I, too, have been wondering how long we can further torture our poor brain-damaged son in order to give him an education. Besides, how much longer can we spend so much money on experiment after experiment, because that's just what it has been—experimenting. It isn't right. It's not fair to push Elliott, and it isn't fair to us. We better start getting used to the truth we have skirted for so long. At least it will help us relax with him better. You're right, Eddie, I'm not going to push so hard any more."

Relief and pain flooded me. Now we both knew what the situation was and we could attempt to deal with it.

Elliott had demonstrated that he knew his basic mathematical processes quite well, he could read with understanding, but he disliked writing. His only true interest in school had been working with tools in the wood shop. Ironically, he did get a thrill from being able to do his spelling well, but his refusal to write rendered this capability somewhat meaningless. Emotionally, Elliott was still trying hard to exert control over himself; he was conscious that a lack of control repelled people rather than attracted them. This disturbed Elliott because his greatest desire was to have friends and be appreciated. To our frustration, he showed no interest in anything academic or vocational. He needed very much to be more relaxed so that his speech could be improved. If only Elliott could concentrate on something of vital interest to him, it would have given him a greater sense confidence. It was so important for Elliott's emotional survival for him to be able to do something well.

A new sheltered workshop had opened up near our home and Elliott was permitted to try working with them for one week. The facility offered jobs for people with assorted physical and mental handicaps. Unfortunately, Elliott's inability to concentrate on the work assigned to him caused the director to dismiss Elliott.

Eddie and I had never discussed institutional care for Elliott, but the idea was creeping into my mind. Nonetheless, I tried my best to fight these thoughts. "Elliott is still young," I would often say to myself. APerhaps we should wait awhile and see what the future will bring."

I had never visited anyone in an institution for either mentally or physically retarded patients. Such state-operated residences held the reputation of being cold, hostile places. I could only visualize old, large cement block buildings housing 100 people huddled into crowded dormitories with only a small recreation room for television or games. In my mind, I guess I was envisioning a facility not much different from a prison, a thought which broke my heart, because Elliott is the kindest, most peaceful man you could ever hope to meet.

But after visiting Farm Colony, a state institution for the retarded in Gainesville, we were convinced that our fears were unjustified. I knew Elliott would be much happier with other young men his own age. The buildings of the institution were old but well-kept. The residential areas were immaculate and clients were dressed in clean, suitable clothing. The staff was warm and receptive and gave us an excellent tour. We had expected the worst, so we were greatly relieved and more relaxed than we had been for a long, long time. Knowing the day would come soon, dreading it, and remembering stories about state institutions, a great tension had built up inside of us. The time had come to place the application.

It was a hot summer day when I took the bus to downtown Miami. As was often the case in those years, Eddie didn't feel well enough to get dressed and drive. As you can imagine, the situation was excruciating for me. My only prior experience at the courthouse was when I had gone

down there to apply for Homestead Exemption on our homes. This time
the trip was different: I was committing Elliott to the State of Florida.

Thoughts filled my mind. Primarily I kept wondering if Elliott
would remain in Gainesville forever? There were no answers. I nervously awaited my turn to see the judge. Finally, I was ushered into his
chambers. The judge was an elderly man, kind and compassionate. He
showed his sympathy with his soft-spoken words and his gentle
actions. He touched my shoulder and explained that it would take
approximately two years for Elliott to be accepted into the program, as
the waiting list was very long and they had only a few vacancies. He
said openings were usually available when a resident died.
Furthermore, he said that parents never took their children out once
they were admitted to the facility.

To some extent, Farm Colony, which was later renamed Sunland, was
a dumping ground for all sorts of defective, deformed, brain-damaged,
handicapped people— from infants to the elderly. Each cottage housed
40 people, according to their age and intelligence bracket, and this is
where they lived, worked, and played together.

My mind was reeling as I bid the judge goodbye and thanked him for
being so kind. On the bus ride home, I continued to weigh the situation.
Even though it was hard to think about the decision we had made, it
seemed that Farm Colony could do more for Elliott than we could at
home. Besides the school and workshop, Farm Colony had a lot of
planned recreational activities. "How fortunate," I thought, Athat parents with normal children do not have to make these kinds of deci-
sions." I thought about the life Eddie and I had planned to live and how
things had turned out. Were we being punished for something we had
done wrong? Why had this happened to us? To Elliott?

Chapter 15

While all of this was going on, Marlene was in the process of growing up. Each morning I would walk her and Maxine to Coral Way Elementary School, the same school that had refused admission to Elliott. Then, for safety reasons—the neighborhood had changed since we'd first moved in—I would go back to the school and walk them home. It was so comforting to see my daughter learning so much so fast. Her report cards were all complimentaryCsuch a contrast to Elliott's reports.

Despite our earlier disappointment with that school, we found Coral Way Elementary to be a very active school with an outstanding principal and an active PTA. Marlene's teacher believed in keeping the students involved in many of the extra-curricular events offered at the school including drama, art, and music. To keep astride with Marlene's interests, I became a PTA member and attended all the meetings. I didn't want to miss out on anything she was involved with. Her normal maturity, which most mothers took for granted in their own children, was a new world for me and I didn't want to miss a moment of it.

I even worked in the cafeteria at lunchtime passing out the cartons of milk and I became chairman of many committees just to keep abreast of ongoing programs. Marlene loved school and was an excellent student.

At this point, we didn't know how long we would have to wait for Elliott to be accepted into Farm Colony. He would pass these days following his routine. In the mornings and afternoons he would ride his bike to Coral Way to visit his merchant friends. Along the way, he would often stop and speak with the garbage men, gardeners, the mailman, the milkman, and anyone else who would pay him some attention. Then he would visit his friend Bill, who ran a small hardware store on Coral Way and Southwest 17th Avenue. Bill sold plants and seeds of all kinds. He was a compassionate man and a good listener. Then Elliott would visit Jack to inspect his latest project. Then by dinnertime, Elliott would head home. Despite these positive contacts, this was a lonesome and uneventful time for Elliott. The need for recreation and a workshop was a dire necessity in our community, but there wasn't anyone with the money and the interest to create such a facility.

Not surprisingly, Marlene kept begging for a sibling, even a cat or dog, to keep her company. Since having another baby was out of the question, we settled for a white Persian cat who we named Snowy. However, Snowy's time with us was short lived because of her terrible allergies. Then Collette, our new white poodle, took Snowy's place. She became Marlene's dog and followed her everywhere. The following spring Collette gave birth to four adorable puppies which we gave to friends.

Then one spring afternoon the long-awaited letter arrived from the State of Florida. They now had room for Elliott and would accept him at Farm Colony in Gainesville. Once again, I was in a state of emotional turmoil. Throughout that day, I tormented Eddie with a barrage of questions: AAre we doing the right thing? Is this really best for Elliott? How can we part with him? What will our lives be like without him? How will he survive without us? Eddie, are we being selfish? Are we making the right choice? Is this best for Elliott?"

It had been one thing to make the application, but it was another to actually be faced with the separation. Eddie and I spent a rather restless, sleepless night as we lived through the decision-making process one more time. Finally, we began thinking rational again as we had before the letter arrived. The storm had passed. Elliott was headed for Gainesville, some 335 miles to the north of Miami.

"We will visit Elliott as often as possible and we'll bring him home for vacations and holidays," Eddie said assuringly. "Rose, we've given him the best education possible and the best medical care available. Now all we can do is hope he'll learn a trade to carry him through and that he will be happy."

The emotional impact of parting struck me so hard that I knew I could not be the one to take him to Farm Colony. Fortunately, we learned that private-car service was available and that other young adults were leaving on the same day.

While taping Elliott's name on his clothes, I explained to him that he would be going to a new school in Gainesville where he would have a workshop in which he could learn to make things. I told Elliott he would make new friends and I assured him that we would visit him often and that he would visit us on holidays.

Morning came warm and clear and I faced the family peacefully and efficiently, making sure Elliott's clothes were ready and his suitcase was packed. We all walked Elliott to the waiting car to join the other children and said goodbye without putting him through our emotional storm. He waved contentedly through the side window and then was gone. Together, Eddie and I slowly walked back into the house. I told myself that I had learned many times it is not good to brood, and once a decision is made, acceptance and involvement in new things is best. With this in mind, I became even busier with Marlene's school activities.

But first there was that first evening without Elliott. This, of course, was a terribly sad time for Eddie and me. I tried to keep my spirits up, but it was difficult. Tears kept running down my face and Marlene kept asking, "What is wrong, Mommy?" As I wiped my eyes, all I could say was, "I am going to miss Elliott very much." I turned away from her as I said, "You will understand this better as you get older." My only consolation was that I felt confident that Elliott would make friends, which had been impossible in our neighborhood. The past years had been so emotional and time consuming; perhaps now was a time for peace and bliss with our beautiful daughter. She would bring joy and laughter into our lives. The tide would be changing, the storm would be over, and the sun would be shining for all of us.

In fact, the next few years were often joyous for us. Everything seemed special, even the simple act of walking with Marlene and her friends while they skipped along. I felt almost as if it were a dream. How great it was to see that not only could Marlene speak well and walk with grace and ease, but she could also run, skip, hop, and jump!

When the time arrived for Marlene to join the Girl Scouts, I took the standard training course to become a Brownie Girl Scout leader, given by the Girl Scout Council of Dade County. Eighteen eight-year-old girls from two nearby schools joined my group, Troop #115. Two assistant leaders helped me. Volunteer mothers and three other women on the committee also assisted me in various duties.

Our many planned activities included the Ayoung people's concert and a Halloween party for which the girls made their own paper costumes and went to Camp Mahachee for a nature hike and picnic. This was a combined trip with another Brownie troop. We stuffed dolls for patients at Farm Colony, enjoyed a nature trip to Matheson Hammock, gathered plants to start a terrarium, and we visited the Crandon Park Zoo. We also toured the local museums and the Fairchild Tropical Gardens, saw a taping of the *Jim Dooly Show*, and had a Mother's Day Tea. The girls wrote and presented a one-act play entitled, "The Mothers, They Forgot." Other times we had dinners at Shorty's Barbecue or went on a hayrides at the Circle B Ranch in Davie. Our family picnic at Crandon Park and a trip to the *Miami Herald* circulation and printing departments culminated our year's events.

Our services to the community were many. Part of each meeting was spent stuffing dolls and animals, making scrap books, and preparing Christmas gifts which were all sent to the Farm Colony in Gainesville, the Mental Health Society, United Cerebral Palsy of Miami, and the Girl Scout Council of Dade County.

Our Brownies were invested again to the intermediate level and became Girl Scouts. But on our final day, the girls announced that they were no longer interested in becoming Girl Scouts. Their interests had changed and they were more interested in boys. And that ended my Girl Scout career. I was sad, but I thanked them anyway. At least they had three years of good citizenship, and learned how to be compassionate for those less fortunate. They gained the love and satisfaction of giving to others, learned about nature, and became better persons. Our Brownie vows were fulfilled and I felt gratified that I had contributed to their young lives.

Meanwhile, in the spring of 1962, Sunland Training Center in Fort Myers opened its doors. At the same time, Farm Colony's name was changed to Sunland Training Center. This meant Elliott could be transferred to Fort Myers. This translated into a shorter trip than we'd been having to make, as Fort Myers was so much closer than was Gainesville. This way, we could visit Elliott once a month. In fact, we visited Elliott the first Saturday after he was transferred to Fort Myers. The newly-painted cottages and roofs sparkled like snow in the sun. The grounds resembled a college campus.

Elliott gave us a grand tour, but we were disappointed to find that there was no air conditioning in the cottages. The sleeping quarters had large fans, but the day room, where the residents ate and watched television, was extremely hot. There wasn't a breath of cool air during the long summer days. My first thought was that we had to get those cottages cooled.

Naturally I got involved in the formation of the Sunland Parents Association and we agreed that our first project was to raise money for air conditioners. As the first president of the association, I decided that we would create a trading stamp fund raising project to raise the necessary money. It took about two years to complete this project, but I'll always be proud of our successful efforts.

As Elliott matured, his desire to work increased. Although his teachers tried to encourage him with various rehabilitation programs, it was difficult for him to feel fulfilled by any of them. Since he rode a large tricycle, Elliott was anxious to do some kind of work in which he could use his bike. He was allowed to deliver messages from one area to another. Elliott was delighted. He was outdoors breathing fresh air, visiting with the people he enjoyed talking to, and earning a few nickels each week. He loved this independence.

In only a short period of time, Elliott had formed some deep friendships with some of the staff at Sunland. His adopted "Papa Hatch" was head of maintenance, and he encouraged Elliott to help him during the day or watch while he and his crew were undertaking heavy maintenance jobs. Elliott absorbed much of what these men knew about tools and equipment. His mind was eager to learn, even though he had always been indifferent to what was taught in the classroom.

Eddie and I were greatly relieved by Elliott's happy adjustment. The dream we had before Elliott left for Farm Colony was coming true. He was happy, safe, and accepted. We had no need to feel guilty that he was no longer living with us.

Sunland at Miami was being built during the two years Elliott spent at Fort Myers. When Marlene and I returned from a vacation in Mexico City, we learned that the new Sunland had opened and that Elliott was to be moved the following week.

His cottage, called "Harney," housed twenty boys. The furnishings were plain, but at least they were new. However, the cottage needed drapes, bedspreads, tablecloths, lamps, flowers, and some decorative touches to make it a home. The center boasted an administration building, a hospital, a developmental evaluation building, a school house, a chapel, a large cafeteria, and a maintenance building. The idea was to provide as much normalcy for the residents as possible. Eddie and I were exultant! After so many years of desperately waiting and hoping for something which had seemed in vain, our prayers were finally answered…or so we believed.

The concept was truly well conceived and the buildings were beautiful. Our Sunland parent group worked to make each cottage a home for our children. After all those years, my interest in active involvement had never waned, and so nobody should have been surprised when I served as the first president of that parent group. As before, Elliott became one of the center's official messengers. His bicycle gave him many hours of relaxation and valuable exercise. His small stature, his thin smooth-shaven face, and his modern eyeglass frames helped create the illusion of a 16-year-old boy, when in fact Elliott was already a man in his late twenties. He could always be seen at a distance from the road as one entered Sunland, peddling on his big bike as if he were a normal suburban child.

His friendliness has always enabled him to meet practically all of the parents who visited their children on weekends and to make friends with a many of the 600 dedicated employees who staffed the center. But Elliott's warmth was not restricted to adults. He made friends with the boys in his cottage, as well as with some of the 1,000 clients in surrounding cottages.

But not everything was perfect. Elliott had his moments of heartbreak. It was a pathetic story of young love. Mary was a beautiful young girl and a victim of mild cerebral palsy. She was almost normal, except for her slight speech and walking impairments. She was very kind to Elliott. He adored her and lived from day to day for the time he would see her. When we shopped on Sundays, Elliott always wanted me to buy a gift for Mary. But after a short period of rehabilitation, Mary was able to adjust to the outside world and get a job, consequently leaving the center and Elliott forever. Mary left was a shattering blow to Elliott. He had hoped to marry her some day. After the initial shock, I explained to Elliott that marriage entailed responsibilities and that he couldn't get married unless he could support a wife. After Mary's departure, Elliott made numerous acquaintances among the girls, and although he seems to have had several crushes, to this day, no one has ever replaced Mary in his heart.

Despite his disappointment over Mary's departure, all in all, things went smoothly for Elliott at Fort Myers. We visited him once a month and usually took him to a motel overnight and part of Sunday. He looked well and since he spent a great deal of time outdoors, he had developed a radiant suntan.

During this time, I became involved in the fund-raising group, Silver Disco, for the Dade County Association for Retarded Citizens. I also became a charter member of the Sunflower Society whose charitable purpose was disabled and handicapped people. Jean and I chaired their Psychic Dinner and Dance. Marlene did all the artistic work on the invitations and table centerpieces, and private booths were provided for the seven psychics who volunteered their services. The event was a huge success and we managed to raise several thousand dollars.

A small group of our friends went on a weekend cruise. Eddie loved this type of travel. His vacations now only included cruises. After going on five cruises, we decided I decided that I'd rather stay on land, so Eddie found a boat mate in Uncle Julius. Eddie usually closed the pharmacy for Christmas week when business was slow and cruised at that time. It was relaxing for him because he didn't have to catch any planes.

Elliott continued to make great progress working in the carpenter shop. He made several footstools which he gave to friends as gifts. He derived a lot of pleasure from making things and giving them away. He was still the official messenger for the center, taking mail and messages from one department to another on his tricycle. He also spent a lot of time with the center's doctor. He constantly complained of headaches or stomachaches just so he could visit the doctor. It gave him another person with whom to communicate. Although this was not the existence I had envisioned for Elliott when he was born, he had finally found himself living a stable and satisfying life.

Chapter 16

When summer ended, Marlene entered the seventh grade at Shenandoah Junior High School, which was only a half a block from our home. Maxine's family had moved into a larger home in Coral Cables, but it didn't take Marlene long to form new friendships and become involved in school activities. I filled my days with the trading stamp collection projects, which took up a good portion of my time. Trading stamps were not the same as green-back dollars, but for me they were preferable for buying a variety of equipment that Elliott and his fellow residents needed.

Sunland employed a highly-qualified professional staff of all disciplines related to the mentally retarded and sufficient personnel to give them the proper care and training in an atmosphere of love and understanding. Many residents at Sunland were rehabilitated completely back into society.

The modern, central air-conditioned center had 53 buildings to implement a program which was considered among the very best in existence. It was constructed on 240 acres of land and resembled a college campus.

While the State of Florida supplied the basic needs for Sunland, donations from groups and individuals paid for much of the equipment and special programs which were enjoyed by the residents. To a great extent, it was these special additions that helped to accelerate the progress of these men and woman.

To our delight, the state had decided that Superintendent Dr. John Presley was going to be transferred to Miami to head the newest center in the state's system. Dr. Presely believed that the development and training of the child took first precedence over any other considera-tions. A special meeting was called for all interested parents to help select the names of the new cottages. The decision was to use the names of the past Presidents of the United States.

The first residents transferred from Fort Myers were from Dade, Broward, and Palm Beach counties. We were thrilled that Elliott was moving to South Florida and of course he was excited to being so close to home. It meant that we could visit him on Sundays and that he could come home for all the holidays and other time he wanted. It was a warm feeling for our small family.

The first important thing on the agenda was the formation of the organization called Parents and Friends of Sunland. Never one to sit back and just watch, I became the association's first president and remained in office for the next eleven years.

The first important project requested by Dr. Presley was the needed equipment for the industrial workshop to provide sheltered employ-ment for 200 trainees. The state was unable to provide this need, but they built the space for the facility. The state funded the buildings, beds, staff, and food, but the comfort items to create a more home-like atmosphere had to come from the public. Our organization raised the initial $1500 and presented it as the first installment with other monies being raised for the center.

Elliott again named himself as the official "greeter." He would park his bike near the entrance of the facility and direct the Sunday visitors to their prospective cottages. In that manner, Elliott became friends with many of the parents and visitors. He also became the official mail delivery man, responsible for delivering mail from one office or depart-ment to another. It gave Elliott the opportunity to spend lots of time outdoors. In the new workshop, Elliott quickly resumed his passion for carpentry. He made small footstools, podiums, picture frames, and many other items.

Merchants Green Stamps provided free publicity for the first stamp drive which netted us a dozen television sets valued at $150.00; each in exchange for 49 filled books of stamps. Once the stamps were collected, we pasted them into books. If they were loose, they were placed in deposit with the stamp company. Stamp accounts were much like bank accounts in those days. We saved and withdrew books as we needed them in order to purchase gifts and assorted necessary equipment. Through a stamp broker we traded a variety of donated stamps for the one brand we were saving. The $2,000 electric organ cost 650 books and the 26 air conditioners were 100 books each.

All of these items added up to about $30,000, which we never could have raised in cash. Fortunately, I found that during the winter season, tourists in the area would give away stamps they were not saving back home. The Matron of the Order of the Amaranth, with its 3500 members, adopted our project as their own and they provided invaluable assistance in our stamp collecting drives.

Around this time, I was featured in the *Miami Herald* with a picture of me wearing a huge collar made of trading stamps. I was named the biggest stamp collector in Miami and the heading read AA New Charity Force." The paper asked for readers to help by sending their stamps or books to my address. I was swamped with the results and had to organize a committee to paste the stamps in books and trade off the books that we could not use.

Meanwhile, Elliott's problems had become less pronounced over the years. He only flared up and lost self-control on rare occasions when someone excited or teased him, but Elliott was living in comfortable and cheerful surroundings, and so such problems were rare.

All the boys in Elliott's cottage called me Amama." They always greeted me each Sunday with, "Hello, Mama" and shook my hand to say "goodbye" when I left. Elliott's last words were always, "Mom, can you leave me a dollar?" I loved leaving him not just one dollar, but two or three, knowing he was happy there and that it gave him joy to have some money in his pocket.

Our Elliott was fortunate. His cottage was occupied by high-level boys with whom he could interact. And even though the state required only a high-school education from the employees, many could easily play the "father" role and soon became "daddy" to the boys. Some residents whose parents visited infrequently were often taken home by these cottage parents to their own homes for weekend visits. To my delight, Elliott's cottage had grown into somewhat of a close-knit family. And because Elliott had become so verbal and personal, was no making friends quite easily. One friend was Ralph, the maintenance supervisor. In fact, I would say that Ralph became like an uncle to Elliott, occasionally taking Elliott home to spend time with his family.

One day I decided to contact the nineteen other mothers from Harney cottage. We met on a Sunday afternoon to collect funds for new drapes for the windows, furniture for the day room, pictures for the walls, and floral arrangements to help make the new cottage in Miami look more like a home. Many other cottages decided to follow our example.

Every Sunday afternoon, Eddie, our white poodle Collette, and I spent time with Elliott. A new shopping center had opened close to Sunland. Elliott enjoyed his treats from the ice cream fountain, and sometimes he would shop for sundry items he needed. Elliott was seeing the outside world and having new experiences. This was more knowledge than all the books at school could teach him. His learning disabilities had been recognized too late. Unfortunately for Elliott and his peers, there was a lack of knowledge regarding how to deal with victims of cerebral palsy, and sadly, this situation has yet to be fully rectified, for each year thousand more like him are being born into the world and thrust upon a system that isn't quite sure what to do with them.

Rose Stosic, one of our mothers, was employed as the instructor of the arts and crafts room. Selected residents who could benefit from her talents were able to come to her class. She initiated the Greeting Card Recycling Project to bring in extra revenue to the center, after which, a concentrated drive for used greeting cards took place. With proper publicity in the area newspapers, thousands of cards were brought in or mailed to the center. The project then enabled the residents to cut the cards apart and paste the front and greeting on lightweight paper to become a new greeting card. A printed stamp was placed on the inside showing that they were made at Sunland, Miami. The cards were placed in packages of 12 and sold for $1.00. The demand was great, as they were much cheaper than the ordinary cards from the traditional card shops. This project lasted several years, until Rose retired and her daughter moved to a group home.

During the years of the crafts class, I was instrumental in securing pastries, cakes and cookies from the Andalusia Bakery in Coral Gables. Before the bakery closed each Saturday at 7 o'clock, I was permitted to pick up half of the leftover baked goods to take to Sunland on Sunday morning. They were delivered to the kitchen to be transferred to the art room on Monday morning. The residents were able to enjoy them for snacks for several days. If the supply was too large, the extra food was distributed in the cafeteria. This routine lasted until the craft department was eliminated for budget reasons.

Another important activity series at Sunland was the Jewish religious classes that were held each Sunday morning under a new Tikvah program sponsored by the Southeast Region of United Synagogues of America. All Jewish holidays were celebrated at the appropriate times by the holiday committee. Passover dinner was one of the favorite holidays. Most of the Jewish parents were very cooperative. We were like a family. The atmosphere at Sunland was very close-knit and informal. Many of us parents were very friendly with the superintendent and staff, and together we worked for the residents, striving to create a sense of community and togetherness that could never be accomplished without our efforts.

Then on May 10, 1971 a most memorable event at Sunland took place. It was a group Bar Mitzvah for ten young Jewish men, including Elliott. AToday you are a man." This familiar commendation, which concludes the Bar Mitzvah ceremony, is the cherished goal of most Jewish boys at age thirteen. When it comes well into adulthood, as it has for these fine young men today, there is a particularly keen sense of fulfillment, said Rabbi Solomon Schiff, director of the chaplaincy service of the Greater Miami Jewish Federation. Ten young men, the oldest being 45, demonstrated their knowledge of the Torah as a qualification for taking on the responsibility of adult Jewish life. Although it was the culmination of three years of study, their knowledge was very limited, and so was the responsibility those men were able to take in the Jewish community because of their mental and physical handicaps. But it was an emotional service, with families and school friends looking on in the Sunland Chapel.

So many of these boys have such a feeling of inadequacy, (as do many of their parents) but this event gave them a feeling that they are the same as others. It gave them a sense of fulfillment that they could never have achieved in sports or scholastic activities. The Bar Mitzvah certificate each boy received was exactly the same as the certificate any other 13-year-old boy received upon completing the course of study and publicly demonstrating his grasp of the foundations of Jewish life. The boys were also presented with a beautiful silver-encased prayer book, which Elliott has cherished ever since. This was an example of the federation's philosophy that the Jewish community believes that the individualCno matter who he or she isCis the rarest, most precious capital resource of our society.

Many Hebrew songs were sung and several prayers chanted. Song sheets were distributed so that everyone could partake in the ceremony. A lavish reception provided by the Parent group in the employee cafeteria followed the services. Publicity in the *Miami Herald* brought the event to the attention of synagogues and the public throughout the South Florida community.

In the fall of 1971, Eddie decided to retire. His health was failing, and even though he wanted to continue working, he had no choice. His surgery from minieres had taken its toll, leaving him with the removal of one ear and left him relying upon a hearing aid in the other. Eddie's retirement was very emotional for both of us. I curtailed all of my volunteer work to keep him company. Collette, our wonderful little poodle, was constantly at his side. Eddie spent time visiting his sisters, Sadie and Esther.

During this time, Marlene was completing her last two years at the University of Florida in Gainesville where she was studying interior design and architecture. In stark contrast to Elliott, whom I'm sure would have been equally successful were it not for his terrible condition, Marlene always excelled academically. Of course I love both my children dearly, but in light of all my struggles and disappointments with Elliott, Marlene has been a particularly rich source of joy and hope, and her very existence has helped sustain me in the good times and bad.

Chapter 17

During 1972, we were deluged with family deaths. Our first casualty was Aunt Tillie, who was stricken with a sudden and fatal heart attack. Uncle Julius was distraught. He sold his home and was planning to live with us in Elliott's empty bedroom. For years, Uncle Julius had been like a father to us and our children were like grandchildren to him, but the remorse of Aunt Tillie's death was too much for Uncle Julius to accept. He and Aunt Tillie had been married for 52 years after all. In short order, his medical problems mounted and he had to be hospitalized. I'm sure that many factors contributed to his death, although the official cause was his allergic reaction to medication he had been prescribed to help cure a skin rash he had developed.

Very soon thereafter, in January of 1973, Eddie began to complain about blackouts and dizzy spells. Initially, the condition was attributed to the ear problems and the subsequent surgery, but then Eddie returned to the hospital for surgery on his carotid artery. To complicate matters further, his shoulder and abdominal pains were diagnosed as a gallstone problem, and this meant more surgery. Then, two days later as he was recovering from the trauma of that procedure, Eddie's heart gave out.

My nerves and emotions were churned inside of me. After 35 years in our close-knit marriage, Eddie was gone and I was left to face an uncertain future. How could I go on? In addition to the loss of my companion, I had lost my economic support. I knew nothing about Eddie's investments and the income from the pharmacy had come to an end. Of course, the painful task of making funeral arrangements was primarily in my hands, but fortunately, this happened when Marlene was home on her semester break, so she was very helpful with all the arrangements. We were advised by the social worker at Sunland that it would be better if we did not bring Elliott to the funeral, that the events of the day would be too emotional for him, and although I've sometimes questioned this decision, I'm confident that we made the right choice in the matter.

In the days and months that followed, Elliott would often call me at home, in tears. "I miss my daddy," he would say. "I miss my daddy."

And I would respond in the only way I knew how. "I miss him too," I would say. "I miss him too."

On the day of Eddie's funeral, the chapel was filled with many of Eddie's customers, as well as the parents of many of the residents of Sunland. Eddie had operated a successful pharmacy business on the basis of his integrity and his philosophy that the Acustomer is always right." His caring and closeness to his many loyal customers, nurtured by years of caring service, proved the inborn qualities of his relationships with people. I knew that our family would not be the only people to miss Eddie.

Despite the countless hours I had spent decorating our beautiful home for our comfort, the time had come for me to move into a smaller home such as an apartment or condominium. After much thought and discussion, Marlene and I decided to sell the house, along with its contents. Because of its ideal location, within walking distance of two good public schools, we quickly had a deal.

At the time, Brickell Bay Club, a beautiful new condominium building on Brickell Avenue, was under construction. It was located in a beautiful setting with a view of the beautiful Biscayne Bay. The building was surrounded by lush landscaping and all the makings of an elegant place. Marlene and I selected one of the two-bedroom apartments. It was very spacious with two balconies with breathtaking view over the water. Because of Marlene's talents with interior design, she had many fresh ideas for decorating our new home. When she graduated from the university in June, she was quickly hired as an associate in a large architectural firm in Coral Gables.

Meanwhile, I continued to work with the trading stamps. At Sunland, one of the craft rooms was dedicated to Aunt Tillie and Uncle Julius Labow for their contributions. Their framed portrait still hangs on the wall today.

After several years, we decided that Sunland's cafeteria looked very shabby and needed a facelift. Of course Marlene offered her services. She drew up plans for turning the area into a modern, up-to-date, beautiful place where the residents could enjoy eating and socializing. Our parent group raised the funds to pay for the redesign and for new cafeteria equipment.

Around this time, however, the State Division of Mental Retardation was gradually becoming aware of the slow progress being made by clients in large institutions such as Sunland. The new system that was being used all over the country for the retarded called for the deinstitutionalization of all state residents. The Division's goal was to reserve Sunland for the severely retarded. Many families, the majority which were middle-aged, opened their homes to Sunland residents who were able to adjust to family life with activities. During the work week, they could also benefit from the access of nearby sheltered workshop facilities.

Some large facilities, housed in either apartment buildings or motels, accepted 40 or 50 of the retarded who did not require much personal attention. I examined some of the homes that were going to open, but I knew that Elliott would not be able to adapt to these surroundings. These facilities simply were not equipped for the handicapped. Such a place would be dangerous for Elliott.

Then we learned that a new group home called Woodhouse, located in Dania, Florida, was going to open in the winter of 1975. This facility was being built to accommodate a small group who wanted to use it specifically for cerebral palsy victims. Woodhouse was located along a canal, so fishing would be one of the activities for the residents living there. Woodhouse consists of two houses that resemble large cottages built side by side. One contains the large dormitory-style bedrooms, complete with new bedspreads, window drapes, and furniture. I was told that each resident would have a new three-drawer chest for his clothes, plus a large wardrobe for slacks, suits, shoes, and other items. The cottage next door houses the living room, offices, a dining area, and a large converted kitchen with new appliances. A large cement patio extends the length of the area between the houses and there are all sorts of trees planted several feet apart. Green shrubs adorn the front of the cottages. In the twenty-plus years that I've been visiting Elliott there, Woodhouse hasn't changed much, and I'm thankful for the stability that this environment has offered Elliott and the others.

From the beginning, Elliott was very happy to move to the Woodhouse group home, which provides a home-like atmosphere, but with the abundance of planned activities. Four of Elliott's friends, also with cerebral palsy, were moved from Sunland along with Elliott. Three of them became his roommates. This new arrangement of having four in a room instead of ten offered the men an increased measure of privacy.

For many years, the United Cerebral Palsy Association of Miami has sponsored a large workshop in its building in the Civic Center area of downtown Miami, but Elliott's sad memories of his father and uncle dying at the adjacent building, the Cedars of Lebanon Hospital, made going there on a daily basis too difficult. I understood his emotions on this matter, and so I saw to it that other arrangements be made right away.

Fortunately, after a brief time on the waiting list, Elliott was accepted into Sundial, a workshop run by the Broward Association for Retarded Citizens, located in Fort Lauderdale. This new facility is located not too far from where Elliott lives at Woodhouse. In order to remain at

Woodhouse, each resident has to have a daily work plan for the five-day week. Sundial offers arts and crafts activities, along with a huge packaging workshop. The workshop offers simple jobs that the clients can easily perform and complete. Sundial is a cheerful, pleasant center operated by a professional, courteous staff.

At the Sundial Workshop, Elliott's hours are filled by stuffing sponges into plastic bags, assembling lamps, and placing computer pins into small oblong containers. His earnings have varied from $3 to $7 per week, a very modest sum, but since this workshop is partially supported by donated funds, each resident is required to pay tuition to make ends meet. In short, the workshop offers Elliott and the others a safe, supervised, satisfying environment where they can be together and be productive.

Unlike a traditional workplace, during lunch breaks, music is piped into the work area and the clients are urged to socialize at their own pace. At times, Elliott has acted as trainer for the new workers. Friendships for Elliott at Sundial have included several teachers, a pretty new girlfriend, several of his follow workers, and the social workers.

In addition to the piece jobs that Sundial Workshop does for industry, they also offer computer classes which Elliott has taken. In a short period of time, Elliott learned to make birthday cards and holiday cards on the computer and he had learned to write and print letters. I have to believe that the relentless effort I made to maximize his intellectual and physical faculties has played a critical role in his ability to adapt to the many changes he has experienced: the moves, the losses, and the new technologies. In a short period of time, Elliott became quite adept at working on the computer, and this continues to be a source of joy and self-fulfillment for him.

So as to further help the residents of Woodhouse develop their creative talents, an arts and crafts teacher was hired to go to Woodhouse several times each week to work with the residents. Elliott always has always had an artistic inclination and he has demonstrated some impressive abilities in the arts and in construction. Once he designed and executed a "dream house" out of cardboard, complete with a brightly-painted interior and exterior. He furnished each room with cardboard furniture and handmade lighting fixtures. Once completed, he presented it to one of his workshop teachers as an anniversary gift. Acts such as this have helped him to cement some fine and lasting relationships at Woodhouse.

"Some people don't realize that it is no disgrace to have a crippled son or daughter. It never really occurred to me to feel sorry for myself. I just wanted to help myself and others."
—Violet Woodhouse

Woodhouse, this wonderful facility, first came about when Violet Woodhouse ran an ad in the fall of 1971. "Cerebral Palsied Adults Need Help. If you can, please attend a meeting at the First Presbyterian Church..."

Responses came in and a group was formed. Mrs. Woodhouse had successfully gathered a group of cerebral palsy adults and in 1967 she incorporated under the name of Crest Palm Residence Hall, Inc. She raised $21,000 towards a building fund and in 1971, the name changed to Cerebral Palsy Adult Home, Inc.

The group's first accomplishment was a tri-county survey of the need for residential placements of Cerebral Palsy adults. Raffles were sponsored in conjunction with luncheons and fashion show benefits. At the quarterly meeting at the church on March 17, 1974, it was learned that this Dania property was under foreclosure proceedings. After much hard work and organization, the title was given to the group on May 15, 1974.

The personal stamina, dedication, and love of Violet Woodhouse focused attention on the needs of the handicapped and provided hope and inspiration to those physically afflicted residents. Thus, Woodhouse became the third non-profit organization in the entire United states to operate a residential home that provided on and off premise training in conjunction with therapy, along with religious and recreational activities to ambulatory and non-ambulatory adults.

It was on February 24, 1975 that Woodhouse received its first six male residents, four of whom are still pioneers of Woodhouse today. They are Gary Bonert, George Carrasco, Billy Gunn, and my son, Elliott Weiss. The capacity has since increased to sixteen residents and for many years, Woodhouse's excellent reputation has resulted in a constant waiting list of about twelve potential new residents. Throughout the years, Woodhouse has had the total support of the First Presbyterian Church, its parishioners, and Mr. Truman W. Worden, the owner of a successful arts and crafts store in Fort Lauderdale, who is a founding member of the Board of directors and is currently Board Member Emeritus.

In short, Woodhouse has come a long way! Driven by its dedication to its Cerebral Palsy adults, the center is blessed with a staff of loyal and selfless employees, some of whom, including Gloria Dixon, the Supervisor/Director, have been working there since the doors first opened.

Woodhouse is a superior-rated facility and has received many accolades from various funding sources, including the United Way, but we are continually looking for ways to provide better services. If we all apply ourselves, we can do more!

> *"We are not all made to go the same speed. Some people run on high-powered motors that don't stop until they burn out. Others must crank their engines to get going, and they never run very fast. Even so, there's a pace uniquely suited to our own temperament, talents, and energies. Life's race isn't always won by those who are swift, but if you help oneself and others you will be richly blessed."*

—*Violet Woodhouse*

Chapter 18

Once Sunland converted its format to custodial care for low-level mentally and physically disabled children and adults, my charitable interests became aimed at Woodhouse. As I grew older and a little tired, my interests became mainly financial. I was no longer interested in attending board meetings or having the responsibilities that come with being an officer. Instead, I established the Weiss Recreation Fund, to which I have contributed money each year. This fund permits the residents to go on tours, the theater, restaurants, and various special events throughout South Florida.

After Marlene got married, I decided to sell the condo and buy a place in an oceanfront building called Surfside Towers, in the town of Surfside, just north of Miami Beach. I felt I'd be more comfortable in a smaller home and I wanted to be closer to Elliott. Furthermore, I had always dreamed of living on the beach, and this was a chance to make that dream come true. It was the perfect relaxation for me. I had waded through so much turmoil in my life. Now was the time and this was the place for me to enjoy long walks on the sand, inhale the ocean breezes, and swim and ride the ocean waves. I would bring Elliott frequently to the ocean so we could enjoy it together.

Over the years Eddie and I had become good ballroom dancers. Now it was time to return to that enjoyable and relaxing social life. I found a few dance clubs and occasionally went out "on the town" as it were.

Some years later, in 1982, I was introduced to Newton Klein, a retired widower who was the father-in-law of my attorney. His wife had died of cancer and he was not happy living a single life. After we had dated for several weeks, I felt that I had found a person who could help me with

Elliott's outings and time at home. Newton was a very handsome man. He dressed well, had a good personality, and seemed very kind and compassionate. It was a wonderful feeling to have someone with whom I could spend my time with. I enjoyed cooking for him and we shared good conversations. He was cultured and courteous. We thought were very compatible and at first we were very happy together.

In May, Newton and I were married in the Rabbi's study. We took pictures and had a wedding dinner at a fine restaurant. The next day we left for Egypt and a cruise down the Nile. Then we spent a week in Greece touring the Greek Isles. It was a glorious trip that I'll always remember fondly.

Because Newton played golf every day, he insisted on remaining in his quarters near the golf course. We quickly sold my beach apartment and moved some of my furniture into his place, and then we upgraded his apartment.

However, as time passed, my interests in Elliott and Woodhouse seemed to disinterest Newton. His grandchildren were so self-sufficient that it was difficult for him to accept anyone who wasn't considered "normal." Our times at home together were fine, but I also had to spend time with Elliott and bring him home for the holidays. After ten months of marriage, I became keenly aware of the differences in our interests and thought it would be best if we divorced and continued in our own directions. Elliott asked me if my divorce had anything to do with him, but I quickly said, "No." How could I hurt my son by telling him that Newton didn't care for him, that he would actually had made fun of him? Elliott's feelings were so deep and he loved everyone. The reality is, I could not accept someone in my life who could not accept and respect Elliott.

And so I returned to my single life and moved into a rental community in Aventura, Florida near the Turnberry Country Club, where I would be living in a small furnished apartment. My new complex had 35 buildings which housed more than 5000 residents. The people there were kind, but most of them were married couples. I joined the social club, but did not find it satisfying socially. The few single women were card players, but unfortunately this was one area in which I had no interest.

Quite frankly, I wasn't sure how I wanted to spend my time, but I knew I needed to find relaxing activities. After so many years of being so actively involved in Elliott's world, I needed to relax my mind a little. In the past I had taken many evening courses in adult continuing education at the University of Miami. Being a spiritual and holistic person, I was interested in psychology, astrology, hypnosis, regression, faith healing with the laying on of hands, and transcendental meditation. Generally, anything that was relaxing helped me cope with my struggles with Elliott.

Happily, at Woodhouse things were going smoothly. The parents of two of Elliott's friends purchased a motorized three-wheeled vehicle called the Little Rascal. After checking out the Little Rascal, I also decided it would be good for Elliott; it would enable him to spend more time outdoors. He could ride down to the waterways, visit people, and make more friends. Elliott quickly learned to guide it and charge it properly. He met many new friends with his "new car," as he called it.

Of course it was not meant to be used on the main streets with heavy traffic, but the Little Rascal was very convenient for getting around. He even used it at Camp Challenge, located near Orlando. This is where all the residents went for two weeks every June. Elliott's Little Rascal could be folded and placed into the van, making it easy for them to transport it to their various trips and outings.

Camp Challenge, funded by the Easter Seals Society, was specifically designed to meet the special needs of the physically and mentally handicapped. The camp was operated by the Crippled Children's Society in Florida for many years. Qualified groups would send children and adults to Camp Challenge for two-week periods during the summer months. The camp was run with professional and volunteer people. The more affluent parents would pay the $800 tuition themselves, while others would apply for a scholarship based on economic need. It was a memorable event for the participants, who would look forward the event each year. The camp provided many of the activities that one would find in any other camp facility. My goal, and the goal of other interested parents, was always, and should always be, to provide the most normal and the most enriching experiences possible for their children.

On that note, one year, as a birthday gift to Elliott, I paid to have a workshop installed on the patio of Elliott's cottage at Woodhouse. For years he had shown such interest in woodworking that it seemed to be just what he needed to fill his spare time. It also filled the gap for his mental energy. Now Elliott had his own cabinets to hold all his tools and a new worktable. To this day, Elliott is a good handyman and often helps with the carpentry repairs at Woodhouse and he always enjoys it when neighbors give him discarded pieces of wood for him to integrate into his projects.

In addition, for about the last five years, an art teacher donated her time to instruct the art-inspired clients to engage in artistic work. Elliott immediately started to paint beautiful winter scenes. In fact, a greeting card company that produces cards made by the handicapped visited the workshop and selected one of Elliott's works, a winter scene, and paid him $300 for the right to reproduce his work on a greeting card. Elliott has also shown a interest in music. He remembers all the popular songs from the years when he was a youngster. From the age of two, he would tap a song out with his fingers and to this day, he can still remember the tunes.

As for Marlene, she was quickly excelling in her career as an interior designer and architect. When searching the real estate market for a vintage home that she could restore, she and her husband found a 1925

Chinese-style home in the Coral Gables section known as the Chinese Village. The large, two-story home had a courtyard, terraces, porches, and a large side yard. The downstairs consisted of a foyer, a formal dining room with a butler's pantry, a large kitchen with a pantry, a powder room, a living room, a music room, and a large screened-in porch leading to a sprawling yard with fruit trees and Oriental trees and flowers. A fish pond on the premises was home to a variety of fish species.

Around this time, I had found a beautiful condominium apartment in Bal Harbour, right on the ocean, so I sold my home at Aventura and moved. I was delighted to be getting back to the beach once again.

Chapter 19

As if my life had been full enough already, in August 1984 my friends Suzanne and Allan purchased Summers, a rock-and-roll nightclub on the ocean in Ft. Lauderdale. We were living close by and I had some time on my hands. Because of her valuable experience from running the office when they had been in the supermarket business, Allan appointed my friend Jean, Suzanne's mother, as the controller and Jean's husband Morris handled the large parking lot across the street. Each day, I would ride in with Jean, then go down to the beach for a swim and some sun. Having nothing else to do, I offered to fold the commemorative Summers T-shirts and put them onto the shelves. Once Jean finished her work, we would go to lunch, go shopping, and then return home. This routine kept up for about a month, and I felt good about doing something constructive again. I guess they liked my "volunteer" work because they offered me the bookkeeping job and was immediately put on the payroll. I was elated. Six days a week I had a place to go and a paycheck to show for my efforts. I couldn't believe it a job! Now, I could afford to do more for Woodhouse. I had not worked for anyone since before my marriage to Eddie. My duties included counting the bartenders' moneybags, writing the checks for the beverage vendors, paying the monthly bills, and of course, maintaining the ledgers.

Unfortunately, in August 1985, I became ill after a year of work. I was experiencing some shoulder pain, which I did not associate with my heart, but after a visit with my cardiologist, I was sent to the hospital with a blocked artery. Although I hadn't felt any severe pain, I learned that I had suffered a heart attack. The surgeon performed angioplastic surgery twice before he could open up the blockage. Then my lungs filled with fluid, and this was followed by a minor stroke. After about a month in the hospital, I was finally released to Marlene's care.

She stayed with me for one week, and then she took me to her home for another two weeks. My recovery was slow because I had lost a lot of weight, but I knew I had to regain my strength and energy. The years of emotional turmoil had finally taken their toll. When I was well enough to walk around, I remember standing before the large mirror in the hallway and thinking how I didn't recognize myself. I had aged so much. What had become of that young, bright-eyed optimistic girl? But don't get the idea that I'm that kind of woman who carries around a lot of regret. I'm thankful that I've been able to accomplish so much over the years for Elliott and I hope I've been a good mother to Marlene and I hope that I was a good wife to Eddie. I think I was. And after all I'd been through, I was just thankful to still be alive.

But I've never been one to give up easily, so once I was able, I took up meditation and yoga. I knew that in order to survive, I had to commit myself to taking a more optimistic view of life. I had to get better. There was still more that I needed to do for Elliott and for Woodhouse. Besides that, I wanted to go dancing again. Once these thoughts began rummaged through my mind, I knew that I was back in control.

During my convalescence in 1985, Jean called to tell me Morris had suffered a stroke and was on his way to the hospital. Fortunately, it was only a light stroke, but Morris was being kept at the hospital for observation, during which time they discovered that he had developed three kinds of cancer; one type was operable, but the other two were not. The prognosis was that Morris would be able to work for a while, but ultimately his case was considered terminal. Surgery was performed in December, and this left him a very ill man. He worked as long as he could, and then he just remained at home, idle.

I spent a great deal of time with Jean, trying to help boost her spirits, but it wasn't easy for her, living with a terminally ill man. Some evenings I stayed with Jean to help bolster her spirits. The next six months were devastating for us, watching Morris, a robust man of 210 pounds deteriorate to a skeletal 95 pounds. My friendship with Jean was strengthened throughout this ordeal, but the days passed slowly and with each day Morris became weaker and weaker. Then finally, the end came on July 3, 1986.

After Morris' death, I spent even more time with Jean because I didn't want her to be alone. I knew that feeling of emptiness, for I had already experienced it with Eddie's death years earlier, and I hoped that my being there would help her through that time.

Naturally, the ordeal with Morris' illness strengthened our friendship. Jean had needed my moral support desperately for those six months and I was there for her as much as I possibly could. Still, I was thankful that I was able to return to work at Summers. I quickly realized what good therapy it was for me to be busy again.

As for Jean and me, our single lives had become entwined. We could plan for just the two of us. Our social interests were very similar since we were both good ballroom dancers. The thought of Jean or Morris ever being single had never crossed my mind. As with Aunt Tillie and Uncle Julius, I mistakenly thought that they would both live forever. Both were healthy, active people. Jean and Morris had raised three beautiful, successful, professional daughters who were in happy marriages and they had been blessed with five grandchildren. Now our lives would take on a new light as we endeavored to explore new challenges.

But I also enjoyed being among the young people at Summers. They were a wonderful group of dedicated men and women. I got to know all about their lives, their girlfriends and boyfriends and all the associated gossip. The environment there was like a family. But by the early 1990's, the City of Fort Lauderdale had grown tired of the annual chaos of Spring Break, and they took steps to urge the college students, and consequently their money, to go elsewhere each year. So as the crowds drifted north to Daytona Beach and Panama City Beach, businesses in Fort Lauderdale that catered to the young crowds began to shut down, and this marked the end of Summers. In 1995, the property was purchased and the building was scheduled for demolition.

By this time, Jean had sold her home and rented an apartment near mine in Bal Harbour. Now we lived only a few buildings away from each other, and since we both loved ballroom dancing, we soon found our niche by joining the Jockey Club. Together, with a gentleman friend, we spent two evenings a week dining and dancing. We were instrumental in the formation of the 60-Plus Singles Club which lasted for about a year. Of the thirteen members in the club, two fell in love and married. We also ran singles dances at two synagogues, as well as other singles groups. This gave us the opportunity to meet new people, but unfortunately we did not meet anyone with whom we wanted to spend our golden years. As it turned out, our membership of forty-two consisted of only two men. Not surprisingly, we decided not to continue with the club.

During this time, Marlene and her husband were having serious marital problems and ultimately divorced, after which, Marlene rented an apartment in my building so we could spend more time together and so that she could seek out new friendships.

Then in March, Jean was introduced to Harry through some relatives who lived in Los Angeles. Harry was a recent widower. His late wife, Sayde Tisch, was the mother of Lawrence and Robert Tisch, the wealthy and famous hoteliers. Harry and Jean were married in December in a beautiful ceremony at their country club. The Tisch family opened a new life for Jean and welcomed her with open arms to their abundant family. They were grateful that Harry had found a wonderful wife and companion, but as a result, Jean and I began to drift apart.

I knew that I must also start a new life, even though I knew it would be painful. Jean and I had a solid friendship of 41 years, but with Jean re-married, I had to form some new friendships and find something to occupy my days. Then Marlene decided to buy a home in Palm Beach to be near her new job, and before long she met Albert, her new-found love, and they married and moved into their new home. I visited Marlene and Albert on several occasions and was impressed with Palm Beach. It was a beautiful city with many landscaped suburban areas. I could not wait until I could sell my home and move to the Palm Beach area myself. The change would be good for me. I'd been living in Dade County for a long time. I needed to experience a new atmosphere, at least for a while.

I sold my condo in a couple of months and I made all the arrangements to move to an apartment in North Palm Beach, not far from Marlene and Albert's new home. But what was I going to do once I got there? I knew I had to find something productive and interesting to do with my time.

I quickly found my "calling" in a framed, handmade antique quilt of silk ties. It was named the "Courthouse Steps" and each row resembled just that. The colors harmonized just perfectly. It was so beautiful. Just gazing and admiring the workmanship was such a pleasure. The quilt had been purchased from a family in the hills of Kentucky. My niece, Shelly, had collected antique quilts for several years and now she had decided to sell them so that she could share these magnificent pieces with the public. Marlene's was one of these prized quilts.

Inspired by these beautiful works, I quickly got it into my mind to get back into business. I began by encouraging the men in my building to donate their unused silk ties, which I then turned into vests, handbags, and ladies jackets. I found a seamstress to help me with the sewing and I made a deal with Jean Frances, a ladies boutique at the Crystal Tree Shopping Center. Immediately, my products were a success and I happily donated my profits to the recreation fund at Woodhouse.

In order to increase my supply of silk ties, I had to turn to the community, and of course, the community came through for me after the

Palm Beach Post, the *Palm Beach News*, and Channel 12 News gave me excellent coverage with stories and pictures about my recycling endeavors. Hundreds of ties were donated as a result, and I received many special orders. After Jean Frances went out of business, I continued selling through a new boutique in Jupiter called Rejean Designs of Palm Beach. The business continued until I moved back to Bal Harbour. I had been enjoying Palm Beach, but I missed living on the ocean and wanted to be closer Elliott.

Chapter 20

Elliott's educational problems stemmed from his learning disabilities. This included attention deficiency hyperactivity disorder. Today these problems are readily recognized in children. Some mental health professionals and educators have mistakenly assumed these children would "grow out of" these disorders, but very often that is not the case.

Behavioral scientists now believe that these disorders are caused by an inability of the central nervous system to produce enough dopamine and norepinephrine, neuro-transmitters required for intellectually demanding tasks such as studying, concentrating, remembering, organizing information, and accurately communicating. Unfortunately, the disorder does not disappear as people become older. People find ways to work around it or disguise it, but they know something is wrong and often feel deeply ashamed, despite their hard-won successes, of what feels like a personal defect.

Behavioral treatment specialists are only now beginning to recognize the impact that learning and attention disorders may have on social behavior among adults. Impulsiveness, explosiveness, disorganization, ease of distraction, chaotic relationships, stimulus-seeking behaviors, and violence are just a few of the symptoms. Often, just recognizing that there is a biological explanation can help to dissipate the shame, fear, and frustration.

It is important to note that an accurate diagnosis is needed and is readily available through testing by a neuro-psychologist, and remedies are now available through psychiatrists and neurologists who are familiar with the psycho-pharmacological treatments for these disorders.

Epilogue

One evening, as Elliott called to tell me about a new girlfriend he met at the workshop, one of the residents was talking very loudly and Elliott could not hear me. Elliott politely told the other resident to please be quiet. Said Elliott, "I'm talking to the best woman in the world, my mother, the lady who made me walk. If your mother would have persisted," Elliott continued, "maybe some of you would also be walking like me." Of the sixteen current residents, only three are able to walk. The others are confined to wheelchairs.

. Sometimes it is difficult to believe that Elliott is my son—the person the doctor said would be nothing but a total dependent, not walking or talking. His movements are slow and unsteady, but he does walk. His speech is a little difficult to understand, but he does communicate, giving evidence of his active mind. This freedom and his mobile legs are the result of years and years of hard work.

From the beginning, as soon as we realized that something was wrong, I refused to let my son live a life of despair. The years of swimming lessons and therapy and special schools were not in vain. He has "all his fingers and toes" and he leads as normal a life as possible for him.

Elliott has never been confined to a wheelchair. His thin legs take him wherever he wants to go. He pushes the wheelchairs of other residents to help them into the dining room for meals or outside for air. He has achieved his most important goal: freedom.

Today, Elliott is an accomplished artist. He works with the computer and excels at carpentry. From donated scrap wood, he crafts podiums, easels, pencil holders, trash bins, and other beautiful items. His workshop includes every tool on the market and he knows how to execute each one of them. He also understands many phases of architecture, and I know that like his sister, Elliott could have been a talented and successful architect. Except for the cerebral palsy, my Elliott could have accomplished anything.

Today, Elliott is a gray-haired man of 60 years of age. He stands about five feet tall and has a thin body. He is a happy, personable, and humorous. Each day his favorite activity is to get on his three-wheeled bicycle and ride down to the Intracoastal Waterway where he visits his friends. Unlike when he was a child, he now has many friends and often gets invited to parties and dinners. Everyone who meets Elliott loves him: the neighbors, his fellow residents, the workshop employees, the Woodhouse residents and staff. But no one could ever love him as much as I have.

Elliott persevered in the hands of good, proficient, experienced people who never would have found Elliott had I not searched them out on his behalf. I brought him into the world, and so it was my responsibility to be his advocate in any way possible. I wanted the best for my son, but given the confusing and difficult circumstances, I couldn't always know what that was. I hope that I made the best choices. I'm confident that most of the time I did.

And for as long as I live, I'll always remember Dr. Carlson's admonition that parents can stifle their children with kindness, when in fact it is discipline and professional guidance that will one day take a person as far as they can go.

God works in mysterious ways. The victories I have helped to achieve for handicapped people like Elliott are perhaps the reason Elliott was given to me. In helping him, I believe that I have helped others. In making his life fuller, I have made my own life more complete.

Printed in the United States
1755